# *The Expressive Edge*

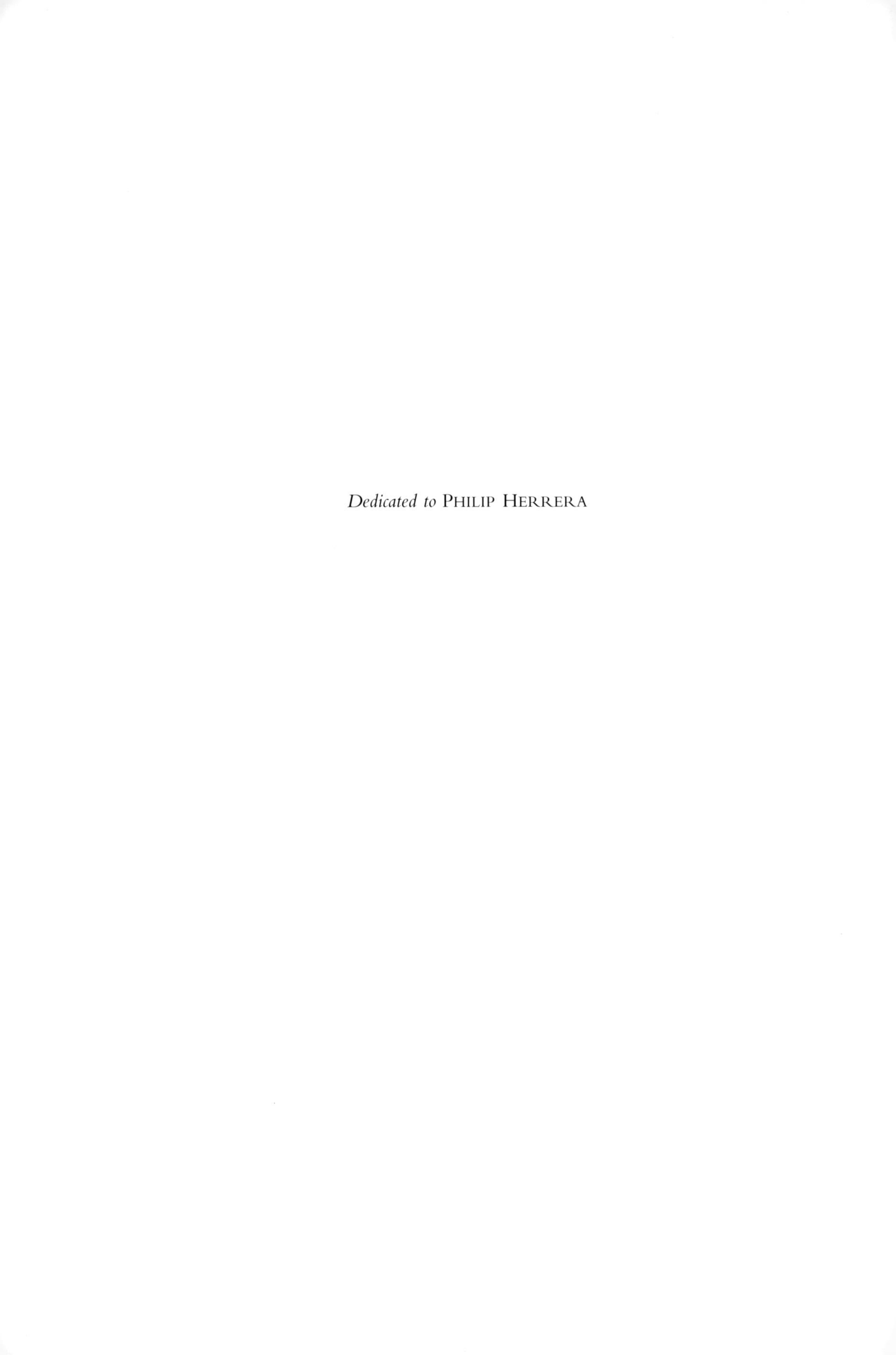

*Dedicated to* PHILIP HERRERA

# Margaret Sheffield

## *The Expressive Edge*

CHARTA

*Design*
Gabriele Nason

*Editorial Coordination*
Filomena Moscatelli

*Copyediting*
Emily Ligniti

*Copywriting and Press Office*
Silvia Palombi

*US Editorial Director*
Francesca Sorace

*Promotion and Web*
Monica D'Emidio

*Distribution*
Antonia De Besi

*Administration*
Grazia De Giosa

*Warehouse and Outlet*
Roberto Curiale



ISBN 978-88-8158-737-7

Printed in Italy

*Cover*
Isamu Noguchi, *The Black Sun*, 1969

*Back Cover*
Gianlorenzo Bernini, *Apollo and Daphne*, 1598-1680



Edizioni Charta srl
Milano
via della Moscova, 27 - 20121
Tel. +39-026598098/026598200
Fax +39-026598577
e-mail: charta@chartaartbooks.it

Charta Books Ltd.
New York City
Tribeca Office
Tel. +1-313-406-8468
e-mail: international@chartaartbooks.it
www.chartaartbooks.it

## AUTHOR'S NOTE

People have asked why I have not included giants such as Richard Serra, Joel Shapiro, or Tony Cragg. The answer is that I have chosen artists whose work gives equal power to Art and Nature, in which Art does not dominate Nature, nor does Nature dominate Art. The edge in these artists' work is the transition point between the two. This is true of the following examples: the crystalline marble edges of the KRITIOS BOY, the flickering, expansive edges of Bernini's APOLLO AND DAPHNE, and the meeting points of earth, air, and sky in Maya Lin's WAVEFIELD.


## MY THANKS TO

Anne L. Peretz and Martin Peretz, Piero Dorazio, Manuela Filiaci, Molly and Gino Mazzone, Bonnie Rychlak, Curator of the Isamu Noguchi Foundation and Garden Museum, Heidi B. Coleman, Photo Archivist, Isamu Noguchi Foundation and Garden Musem, Peter Rauch, Blair and Paul Resika, Nancy Azara, Michael McGinnis, James R. Sheffield, Ann C. Sheffield, Francesca Mannoni, Diane David, Fronia Simpson, Pete Marinucci, and Giuseppe Liverani with the staff of Charta.

*Margaret Sheffield*

*Maillol's sculpture has the ripeness of a plump fruit,
which makes me want to reach out and touch it.*

HENRI MATISSE, 1905

*I feel I exist on the boundaries. Somewhere between science and art,
art and architecture, public and private, east and west. I am always trying to find a balance between these opposing forces, finding the place where opposites meet. Water out of stone, glass that flows like water, the fluidity of a rock, stopping time. Existing not on either side, but on the line that divides. And that line takes on a dimensionality. It takes on a sense of place and shape.*

MAYA LIN, 2000

## *Contents*

## *Chapter I*

# EDGE AGAINST SPACE

Sculpture, in a way we cannot quite explain, is much harder to look at than painting. Many art historians, even the very best, struggle with sculpture. What does sculpture have that painting does not? I should say that I am not, here, including the fusion of painting and sculpture in installation art or video art. First and foremost, sculpture's edges are three dimensional: they don't exist on a flat surface, but work against space.

This book attempts to explain the beauty of sculpture through the sculptural edge. A sculptor's energy and signature style come as much from the edges as from the core. The incitement to write about edge in sculpture was inspired by a conversation with Meyer Schapiro about edges in painting and, a year later, by interviews with Isamu Noguchi about edge or plane in Eastern aesthetics[1] (p. 23). In my interviews with Noguchi, we talked about how his articulation of edge and plane derived from the Zen aesthetic principle that holds that beauty resides in primal, non-geometrical forms, with their asymmetrical edges relating to indeterminate space.[2] This idea of edge against space strikes me as a remarkable idea, both visually and philosophically, and it has caused me to look at the work of sculptors of all ages in a different way. To me, a sculpture's unique rhythms and movement—whether Michelangelo, Bernini, Boccioni, or Maya Lin—lie in the fluid dynamics of edge, "edge" including surfaces, projections, contours with volume and silhouettes.

I have observed that sculpture has essentially three kinds of edges. These are not airtight categories: they often appear in combination. These three kinds of edges—and/or their combination within a single work of art—are clearly visible to the eye yet exasperatingly tricky to define verbally.

They are nonetheless useful for analysis:

1. Edges that contain, such as seen in ancient Greek sculpture like the KRITIOS BOY (p. 25) or in modern classicists like Aristide Maillol (see p. 27, THE MEDITERRANEAN).

2. Edges that expand, as with Gianlorenzo Bernini's APOLLO AND DAPHNE[3] (p. 28), Michelangelo's *non-finito*[4] in the Florence Accademia di Belle Arti ST. MATTHEW (p. 30) and the CAPTIVE (p. 31), and with Rodin, in his work MIGNON (p. 29), an example

of what the artist called his "multiple silhouettes." All the above are examples of the "expanding edge."[5]

3. Edges which dissolve or are in constant flux, as in contemporary sculptors like Maya Lin and Jian Jun Zhang.

Meyer Schapiro's concept of "the incomplete" in great works of art, as stated in his essay "On Perfection, Coherence, and Unity of Form and Content" (1966), is critical here, in regard to both the content and the style of each artist. Schapiro asserts that "great works of literature, painting, and architecture are incomplete or inconsistent in some respects. And one might argue that in the greatest works of all such incompleteness and inconsistency are evidences of the living process of the most serious and daring art."[6]

This book will show a connection between the life-giving energy in incompleteness, the Zen aesthetic about imperfection, and the constant flux of edges in contemporary art.

Edges, both contours with volume and silhouettes, serve an incompleteness that the artist wants to suggest: this incompleteness runs the gamut of Michelangelo's celebrated *not-finishing*, Noguchi's concept of the "imperfect," and Penone's concept of nature—as-becoming in the changing "empty" spaces of RESPIRARE OMBRA (p. 86). Even when the edges themselves are not clear and linear it is chiefly through the edge that the art expresses its flowing life. The empty spaces in Penone's wire-mesh cages of RESPIRARE OMBRA are continually "completing themselves" or are in a state of becoming. Jian Jun Zhang's works include cast stones made of ink and resin that were gradually eroded by water, recycled through the work's spout until the clean water and the solid ink and resin stone had become one dark pool. The idea of "incompleteness" was inherent in these works' conception.

For these contemporary artists—as before for Bernini and Noguchi—water, though seemingly "immaterial," is a powerful transformational material, as strong as marble or granite. Maya Lin's fountains combine granite and water; the water falling over stone steps in Lin's CIVIL RIGHTS MEMORIAL (p. 98) recalls Noguchi's many fountains.[7]

Forceful, eternal, and elusive, water is a boundary which we do not truly grasp visually. It is the apparent "edgelessness" which bewitches Lin when she writes in her book *Boundaries*: "I stared at the ocean for hours, trying to find a beginning and an end. But of course there is none." In the work of the Chinese-American sculptor Jian Jun Zhang, water is a prime element: he uses water as the anti-monumental yet eternal force which erodes the ink rocks.

Each sculptor chosen for inclusion here has asked the question: "How can a work of art that is permanent, express the ever-changing power of nature?" All would answer: "Through the edge."

This book looks for meanings of particular kinds of edges and how their purpose changes from one period to another. For example, the ragged and irregular edges of Rodin's L'HOMME QUI MARCHE (p. 40) evoke muscular, sensuous energy, whereas the raw edges of Noguchi's LANDSCAPE TABLE SCULPTURE are suavely elegant and part of the artist's philosophy of nature.

Edges and boundaries are crucial to each sculpture's formal aesthetic beauty and the sum of contours and edges creates the force of singular rhythms in each work.

People have asked why I have not included giants such as Richard Serra or Tony Cragg. The answer is that I have chosen artists whose work gives equal power to Art and Nature, in which Art does not dominate Nature, nor does Nature dominate Art. The edge in these artists' work is the transition point between the two. This is true in the following examples: the crystalline marble edges of the KRITIOS BOY; the taut bronze volumes of Maillol's THE MEDITERRANEAN, the flickering, expansive edges of Bernini's APOLLO AND DAPHNE; the violently mobile surfaces of Rodin's bronzes such as L'HOMME QUI MARCHE; the mobile, elusive "edges" of Penone's SCRIGNO (p. 61), and the meeting points of earth, air, and sky in Maya Lin's WAVEFIELD (p. 68).

In every work, the sum of contours and edges creates unique rhythms. The heightened vitality of rhythm, largely the result of the artist's orchestration of internal lines and outer boundaries, is the pulse and energy of aesthetic beauty.

I find dictionary definitions of "edge," "contour," and "boundary" frustratingly vague, as they change from one dictionary to the next. One meaning of edge, "a dividing line, or line of transition from one state or condition to another," is seldom applied in ordinary English usage but it is this meaning—as a line of transition from edge to space—that has inspired this book.[8]

Surface edges are usually called surface textures; I call them "edges" because they are sharp and projecting, and have dimensions up to 3, 4, or 5 inches, such as in Rodin's GATES OF HELL, which encompass edges on an epic scale. One of the most amazing examples of a marble edge carved both as outline and surface are the delicate perimeters of Prosperina's tears in Bernini's famous PLUTO AND PROSPERINA in Rome's Galleria Borghese.

Just as definitions seem inadequate, the effects of edge in sculpture are as difficult to pin down as those in painting, but with one difference. The effects in painting have been described and discussed; while critics and art historians have commented on the effect of edge in painting, the same emphasis has not been given to sculpture. John Golding, for example, writing about Cézanne, observes that "the dark blue contours reaffirm the outline of the figure, but simultaneously, they open it up into space and into the surrounding environment."[9] Robert Hughes has written of how difficult to perceive and to "fix" Morandi's forms because of their mutable edges.[10]

As I talked to friends and colleagues about sculptural edges, I came to realize that most people think of them as geometric, like the edges of a carton or the curve of a ball. It surprised many that an edge could have irregular, sensuous textures, as in a Japanese Raku bowl, that refuse to conform to rectangle, circle, and triangle forms. Joel Shapiro's sculpture shows the artist taking "static" geometrical forms as units of the work, but combining them in a way that is dynamic, asymmetrical, off balance. The sort of edge found in the work of Lin or Zhang, or Giuseppe Penone—watery, cloud-like, or evanescent—is unfamiliar to most people. Yet as Penone shows in his work, even human breath has dimension and an edge, no matter how diaphanous or invisible.

In sculpture, edges are the means by which emotions are externalized. In flesh-and-blood arts, the viewer kinetically experiences the contours of the dancers' bodies. A dancer friend expresses it this way: "Every time we create a movement, not only the edges of our bodies change, but our feelings, our thoughts as a result of that change in physical edge."

What I have called the "dissolving edge" is perhaps the most difficult to define. Sometimes the effect of a multiple edge calls for the word "flickering" (as in Bernini) and sometimes the word "dissolving"; obviously these words are not "precise" definitions but poetic approximations. Among the most celebrated examples are Rodin's figures; here we experience an almost palpable kinetic awareness, which mirrors an inner emotion.

This points to an essential difference between sculpture and painting, the degree to which it is kinetic and tactile as well as visual. With a kinetic awareness, we experience the action of the work, whether it is in Bernini's DAVID (p. 80) or Boccioni's UNIQUE FORMS OF CONTINUITY IN SPACE (p. 84).

Bernini's famous fountain sculpture, FOUNTAIN OF THE FOUR RIVERS (p. 81), in Rome's Piazza Navona, has a swashbuckling, three-dimensional force: we are irresistibly urged on by the gods' gesturing limbs, to encircle the gushing fountain just as they do. Similarly, Rodin's L'HOMME QUI MARCHE makes us kinetically aware of the strangely combined muscles involved in the action of striding.

To the great German art historian Johann Gottfried Herder, sculpture appeals to our sense of "touch," as painting appeals to "sight."[11]

With the "tactile," for example in Rodin's bronze MIGNON, we experience—even if we cannot literally touch it—every passionate ridge of bronze in his lover's windswept hair and open mouth. Albert Elsen comments on the BURGHERS OF CALAIS: "within an area confirmed by a few inches of the sculpture, each fingertip will encounter surface inflections of a different character." As described by Albert Elsen, "seen under strong sunlight, studied by itself, the drapery reveals an alteration of projections and almost brutal incursions into shadow, along with subtle deviations from the perpendicular."[12]

Sculpture is also corporeal. It has a capacity to capture a momentary pose, gesture, or gaze. Examples of this are the gaze of Bernini's LOUIS XIV (p. 83), or the struggling figure of Daphne in Bernini's APOLLO AND DAPHNE. The viewer physically identifies with the figure and imagines his or her own capacity to inhabit that pose.

In Benvenuto Cellini's PERSEUS (p. 57) the corporeality enables a voluptuous physicality of stance and energy. Cellini's subject is partly a muscularity that convinces the viewer of Perseus's intention to behead Medusa; the viewer feels volition in the figure's hips and buttocks. An example of contemporary corporeality is Maya Lin's VIETNAM VETERANS MEMORIAL, a polished granite edge seemingly carved into the earth. The artist said her intention was to "take a knife and cut open the earth" so that the viewer would feel the finality of death.

The visual truths of edges/contours are elusive. We think we know what edges and boundaries are, yet they are difficult for most of us to grasp and "see." The volumetric "edges" within a certain area of, for example, a muscular torso by Michelangelo or Rodin occur within the outer boundary; within the outer edge are internal edges, or, as Kenneth Clark says, "lines with mass." This is what is hard to see, to experience, and to define, which is why Clark and others are at a loss to do so. In "The Art of Seeing," what Jed Perl calls "art's endless peculiarities" are most manifest in its edges which are a key to art's energy and unity.[13]

Looking at sculpture, we think we see a single contour, but in fact see a series of subtly varying edges, which change as we move. The contour, in effect, is more like a bridge to the surrounding space, or like a membrane, that allows the edge to work against space. This strongly resembles the thought implicit in the Japanese word for edge—*hashi*, meaning a bridge between one world and another.[14]

Essential to the beauty of contours is their creation of unique rhythms and moods. In contrast to the calm majesty of the KRITIOS BOY, or Maillol's THE MEDITERRANEAN, where contours are slow and the focus sharp, in Bernini's APOLLO AND DAPHNE, the tempo increases, the edges are violently active, with an intense, mind-bending rhythm. Unbridled rhythmic force compels every one of Bernini's modulations in the body of DANIEL IN THE LION'S DEN and the drapery that swirls sensuously around it. These liquid rhythms create indelible images, and, as in music, a heightened sense of life.

Classical Antiquity, in continuing the tradition of carved stone, sanctioned the preference for the cube or block of stone, which persisted until the Renaissance. This static and contained outline of the figure is echoed by the contained nature of the marble block. Thus, the lines and contours of figurative forms occur within a geometric shape. Conversely, the marble or stone cube's outer shape is mirrored by a more or less geometric arrangement of the body in an outline that is not agitated but restful. In contrast to Bernini's baroque exuberance of contour is the RIACE WARRIOR (p. 59) or Maillol's contour of restraint.

To be expressive, edges do not have to be flamboyant. Classical sculpture overpowers us with quiet balance, its rhythms slow and detached. For example, the RIACE WARRIOR moves us because the contour or edge "contains" an entire world of feeling and thought. In the case of a Skopas athlete, by contrast, the aesthetic has changed to a more theatrical one, with quicker rhythms and twisting contours. Works such as the LAOCOON of the early first century BCE, push sculpture away from the containing classical edge towards the expansiveness of the Hellenistic and the Baroque.

In Western figurative sculpture, a tantalizing visual puzzle is the relation of pose to contour. Rodin observed that in order to convince the viewer of a bodily action, the sculptural pose must suggest two actions. An example of this is L'HOMME QUI MARCHE, where the artist combined two actions in one—an active forward movement in the torso and a passive backward movement of one leg—to achieve this effect of verisimilitude.

The contours of Rodin's sculptures—which change from his early works where contours are "containing" to later works where contours are multiple and "expansive"—result from realistically observed poses, whereas those of classical Greece result from idealized poses. The successful pose conveys to the viewer a bodily sense of invisible, visceral energies—muscles contracted or relaxed—suggesting ideals, moods, and energy.

Greek sculptors had to understand how the contours of marble or bronze might convey life. The planes of a form create the three-dimensional object; the nude body or other sculptural objects are a series of planes that spiral around a central core.

Qualities of classical sculpture also exist in the modern period, as, for example, in that great modern classicist Aristide Maillol. Matisse once said about Maillol: "We never discussed sculpture, for we could not understand each other. Maillol worked in masses like the ancients, and I worked in arabesques like the Renaissance sculptors. Maillol's sculpture has the ripeness of a plump fruit, which makes me want to reach out and touch it."[15] Due to the subtle balance of center and contour, in Maillol's nudes the legs, chest, and arms work together; there is a containing edge which makes the volume seductively tactile.

What we may call the "dissolving" edge can be found in Michelangelo's CAPTIVES and decades later, the late PIETÀs. In the CAPTIVES, Michelangelo transforms the knots of muscles into ferocious or tragic metaphors for human struggle. Michelangelo's *non-finito* is largely what creates this: the roughly chiseled and pitted marble makes a clear contour or outline impossible.[16]

Before Michelangelo, the early Italian Renaissance master Donatello is one of the first in Western art to have explored the expressive possibilities of edge and surface in both marble and bronze. As the scholar Charles Avery points out, the rough and unfinished surfaces of the bronze relief of Saint Lawrence in the church of San Lorenzo are visual corollaries to the savage subject matter.

For a long time the "dissolving" edge in Michelangelo's roughly carved passages were thought to be unfinished, as the artist had not smoothed over rough, irregular surfaces with a pumice, perhaps because he was overburdened with the Sistine Chapel ceiling. These celebrated edges manifest as myriad tiny dots from chisel marks in the marble block, which refuse to configure into a single clear contour. Questions lingered. Were the rough passages in the two late PIETÀs intentional, or had Michelangelo intended to polish them at a later date?

In the CAPTIVES or the RONDANINI PIETÀ (p. 33), the irregular chisel marks create "dissolving edges" that are variants of what we have called the expanding edge. The modeling of the ST. MATTHEW, with its roughly chiseled edges, is another example of Michelangelo's deliberately "dissolving" marble surfaces. The rough carving intensifies the struggle of this figure. Perhaps the most breathtakingly beautiful example of Michelangelo's deliberate use of raw, roughly chiseled stone to express suffering and excruciating loss is the RONDANINI PIETÀ. This work was begun in the mid-1550s, and according to contemporary sources like Vasari and Daniele da Volterra, the artist was working on the Pietà when he died at the age of eighty-nine. Here the uncertain contour edge, the myriad chisel marks of surface edges, and the interior rhythms are outstanding for expressing a sense of the broken body in pain. Perhaps more starkly and inarguably than in any other work, Michelangelo reveals himself as a deeply religious person who profoundly felt the suffering of the Madonna and her dead son.

Clearly these projections and indeterminate contours are not literally dissolving, like the watery edges of Maya Lin, but the words are suggestive, evocative of their meaning. This goes back to the reason sculpture is hard to talk about, as the words we use seem inadequate or do not truly define the subject which is physical, tactile, kinetic.

Perhaps the greatest, most subtle difference between sculpture and painting is the sculpture's empathic potential. With our precious human capacity for empathy, we can experience physically and spiritually the tactile as well as the mental experience of suffering. The edges of bulges, ridges, projections, and concavities, has made the viewer think he or she is physically touching the literal "skin" which, in its "rough" (rather than smoothed) state, is symbolic of the process of pain and torment. In Michelangelo's raw and unfinished edges, he conjures a skin that is intensely painful and that reads to the viewer as an "open wound." In his roughly chiseled Madonna in the RONDANINI PIETÀ, he invites us to physically and mentally experience Mary's loss. It is hard to find a figure in the LAST JUDGMENT where the beholder may feel the reality of pain as much as in this sculpture.

According to Vasari, Michelangelo attacked this Pietà and undid it by cutting away the torso and the head of the Christ to reveal an emaciated figure fused with the elongated figure of the Mother.

This outstanding range in the meaning of "raw and unfinished" as opposed to "polished" is clear when one contrasts the abstract elegance of Isamu Noguchi's carefully orchestrated "broken" edges with the roughly chiseled edges of Michelangelo's religious PIETÀs in sixteenth-century Florence. The same stone-carving techniques were used for such different expressive goals: Noguchi's to convey an Eastern view of edge as a bridge to the "metaphysics of nature" and Michelangelo's unpolished edge used to convey anguish and suffering.

We note again here the similarity between the primal energy of the incomplete as *non-finito* and the Zen aesthetic of art's imperfection as giving life to the work of art.

In the contemporary world, Magdalena Abakanowicz, as in NEGEV (p. 101), chooses to create an irregular edge to express what she calls the "confession of nature's powers. The texture of the broken granite, like the trunk of a tree or human muscles, is nature's confession to man."[17]

The sensational 1506 unearthing in Rome of the Hellenistic virtuosity LAOCOON AND HIS SONS had a great influence on Michelangelo, and sparked the move away from the containing edges of more classical High Renaissance aesthetics towards the Baroque's explosive energies. The central figure—the twisting, imprisoned torso of the father—inspired the poses of Michelangelo's CAPTIVES, both by its compelling image of strain, and a muscular, spiraling shape, which the sculptor was to recommend to artists as a haunting flame-like movement.

Michelangelo was not the only genius to follow the LAOCOON's contours in his works. Later, Gianlorenzo Bernini in his DANIEL was to invent poses that echo both the LAOCOON and the flame-like movement of Michelangelo's CAPTIVES. But in Bernini, the contour of Daniel's torso has softened into the melting form of the prophet in prayer.

The holes and bumps in Rodin's surfaces—which I call "surface edges"—are deliberately unfinished, because he recognized that fissures in the bronze are crucial in the expression of nature, light, and life's energy and tumult.

As we have seen, Noguchi's basalt "landscapes" are pitted because of an aesthetic which values the imperfect for being closer to nature's non-geometric indeterminacy. In Lin's WAVEFIELD, the open-ended, infinite contours are symbolic of universal extension. To Abaknowicz, the texture of the broken granite shows a power in nature equal to that of art. Robert Lobe's monumental, irregular edges and volatile irresolutions are carefully crafted symbolic ideas.

Our twenty-first-century aesthetic is certainly that of the dissolving, and open-ended, as in the mutable indeterminate edges of Giuseppe Penone or Maya Lin, which echo the Renaissance *non-finito* and the flickering contours of Bernini's Baroque. Rough contours, in constant flux, like those of Maya Lin, often symbolize themes of emergence. The presence of the mind of the artist in an unfinished passage—whether the artist be Michelangelo or Noguchi—adds a layer of real-time experience for the viewer who can imagine the narrative of the sculpting act, whether it is in the additive process of modeling clay or the subtractive one of cutting stone. At their most darkly expressive, the pitted damaged edges in Michelangelo or Abakanowicz may express anxiety, alienation, and suffering.

In Rodin's L'HOMME QUI MARCHE, two kinds of edges—seething, volatile surface edges and complex, multiple outer contours—create the whole work of art. Precise examples of "surface edges" are in details of MIGNON, and L'HOMME QUI

MARCHE. For the viewer to comprehend what Rodin has achieved takes time and close attention. Without every single variation on its surface and the hard-to-grasp, multiple outer silhouettes, as well as the interior movement of rhythms, the sculpture would not have the preternatural force to lure the viewer back again and again.

In Noguchi's VERTICAL VIEW (p. 85) and LANDSCAPE TABLE SCULPTURE the pitted and carved irregularities of edge—created by the very same tools as Michelangelo's—evoke themes of emerging form. Noguchi's edges cohere into an elusive, non-geometrical unity, close to what the artist called "the metaphysics of nature."

I have asked myself if there is any connection between Noguchi's vision of edge, which is philosophical and poetic, and that of Giuseppe Penone, Maya Lin, Jian Jun Zhang, and Robert Lobe. And what, if anything, connects the contemporary artist's view of edges, whether contour or surface texture, to those of Archaic and Classical Greek, Renaissance, and Baroque sculptors, to Rodin, and the Futurist sculptors. Certainly the traditionally recognized attributes of sculpture—corporeality (or mass or volume), weight, tactility, and kinetic perception—are absent from sculptors such as Penone or Maya Lin.

In Penone, Lin, and Zhang, contours are in constant flux. We see that their edges are mysterious, conjuring phenomena such as breathing, water, and the passage of time.

Much art which dominates the present moment is, like the installations of Sarah Sze and Pipilotti Rist, a fusion of painting and sculpture or, as it is often called, "installation art." Why is this? A devastating universal effect of the computer has been to devalue the three-dimensional. Things have flattened out, dematerialized. Although we exist in three dimensions we seem to now see in only two dimensions. Art teachers tell me that students prefer to look at flat slides rather than going to experience a three-dimensional sculpture. As the choreographer Fédéric Flamand was quoted recently in *The New York Times*: "With the computer we are in front of a screen, but not in front of a body. Where is the body in all this?"

Sze works in architectural spaces and chooses everyday, seemingly random objects (Q-tips, pieces of paper, small video projectors) to actify the space. What results is a fluid cascading of objects which, as they pour forth and whirl, create edges which drastically dissolve.

Pipilotti Rist's POUR YOUR BODY OUT (7354 cubic feet, 2009) at New York's Museum of Modern Art had an immersive flow of images on a vast scale. Rist's nerve and panache are legendary: POUR YOUR BODY OUT is a tour de force, with colossal pigs biting into fruit, menacing hunks of matter, and other images of ongoing life processes. Whereas other artists in this book gave Art and Nature equal powers, Pipilotti Rist shows the anarchy of a heavily terrestrial Nature. Like a giant tsunami wave, the energies of life devour edge after edge, hurling images to a height of 25 feet above the viewers' heads.

Rist and Sze are dramatic examples of how contours which dissolve dematerialize as they overlap. If Rodin's edges signify passion, and Noguchi's a link to the metaphysics of Nature, then the multiplying contours of Pipilotti Rist relate less to nature and art than to the self. In Rist, the viewer cannot apprehend the space around the object because the viewer is immersed in the object. Rist's work exists at an extreme opposite to the dimensional sculptors in this book. But in her gleeful and disorderly exaltation of flux, there is an affinity to the aesthetic of the incomplete in other dimensional artists.

Maya Lin's new STORM KING WAVEFIELD, which opened on May 9, 2009, is the most spectacular and revealing example of contemporary sculpture's expressive edge. This vast earthwork, while changing in contours, is also both three dimensional and permanent. Created with waves of earth over a preexisting gravel pit, the artist then planted the earthen edges with indigenous trees and flowers. Deliberately immersive, changing in relation to the viewer, STORM KING WAVEFIELD has both the permanence of the three-dimensional and the ephemeral of today's art.

The power of the sculptural edge continues to be its capacity to express the dynamism that is inseparable from life.

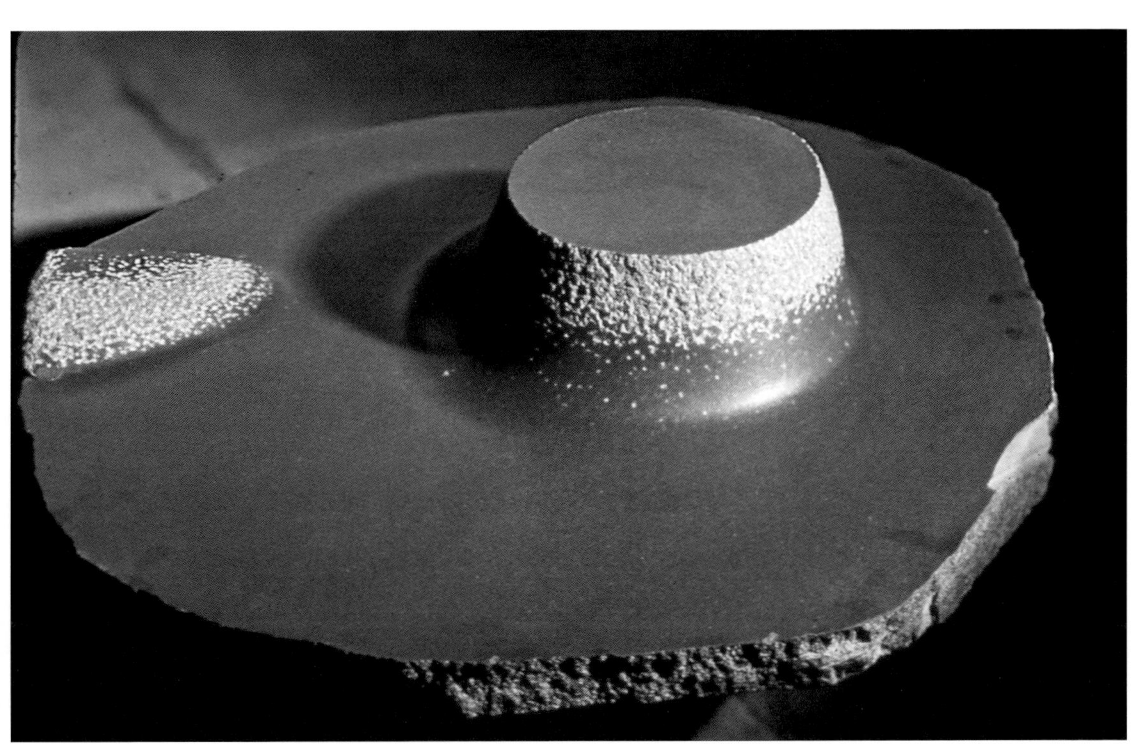

Isamu Noguchi, LANDSCAPE SCULPTURE, late 1960s

THE CONTAINING CLASSICAL EDGE: THE KRITIOS BOY

*Within the crystalline marble outline of the Kritios Boy, rhythms are slow and the focus sharp. The edge contains volumes that are taut and complete.*

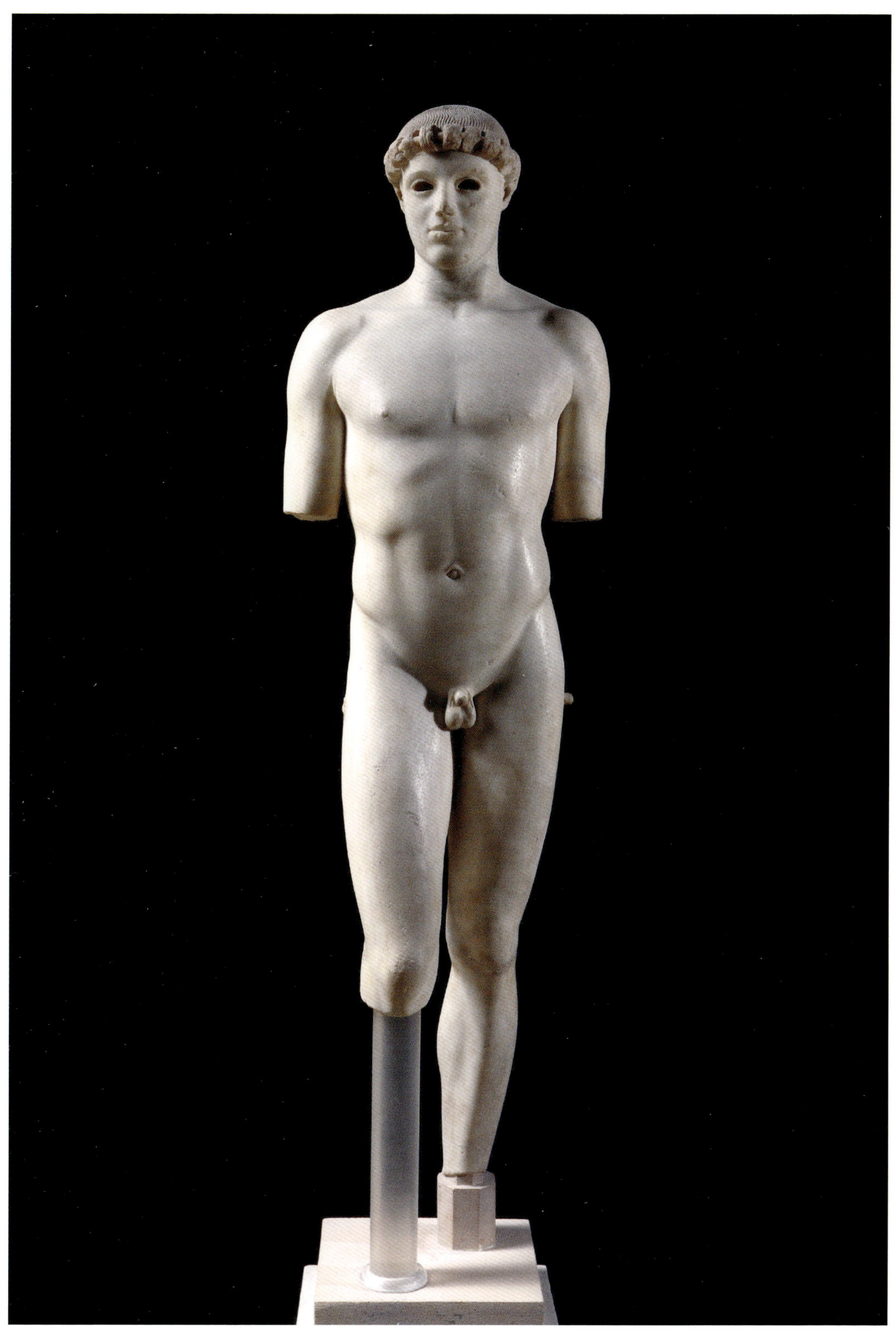

KRITIOS BOY from the Acropolis, ca. 490–480 BCE

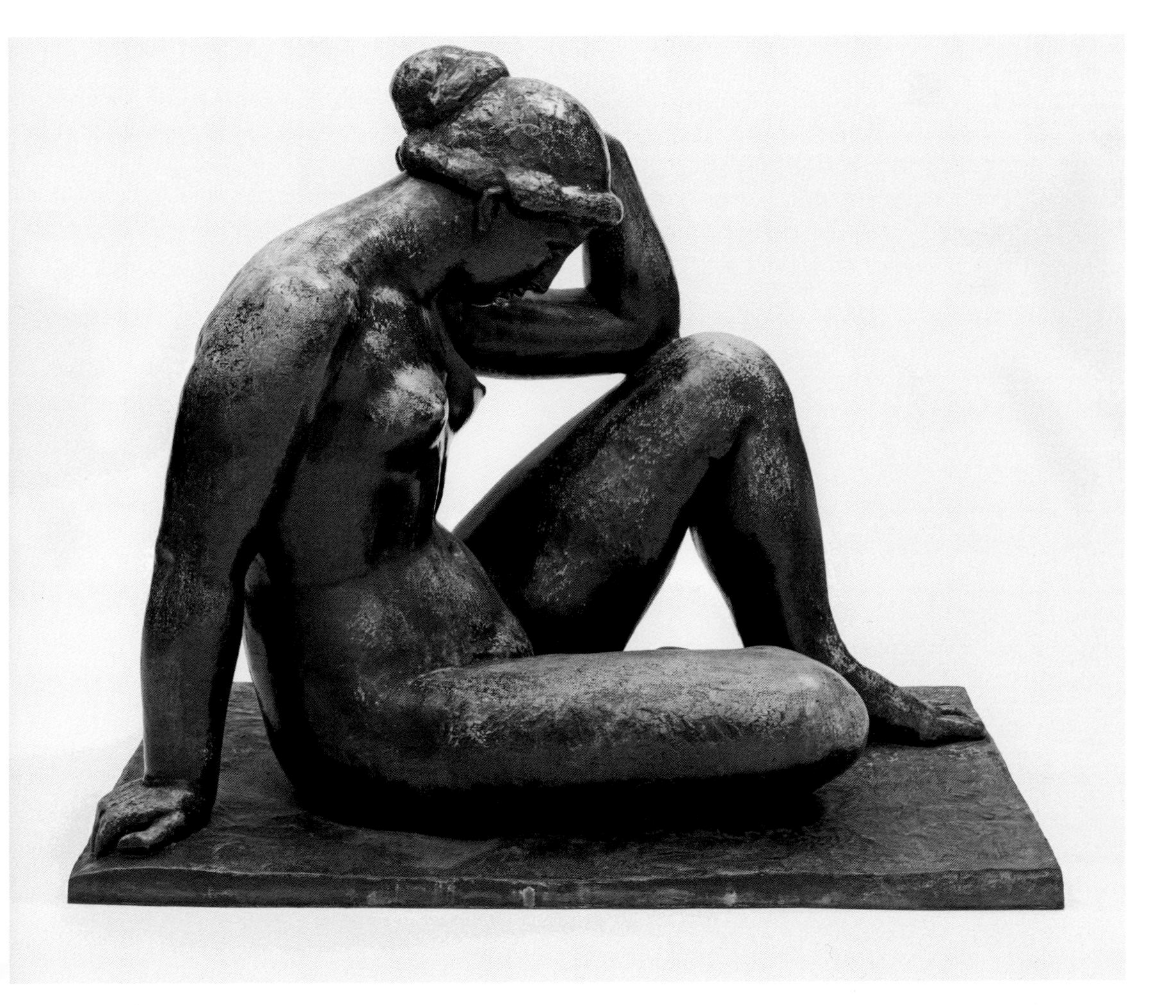

Aristide Maillol, THE MEDITERRANEAN, 1902–1905 (cast 1951–1953)

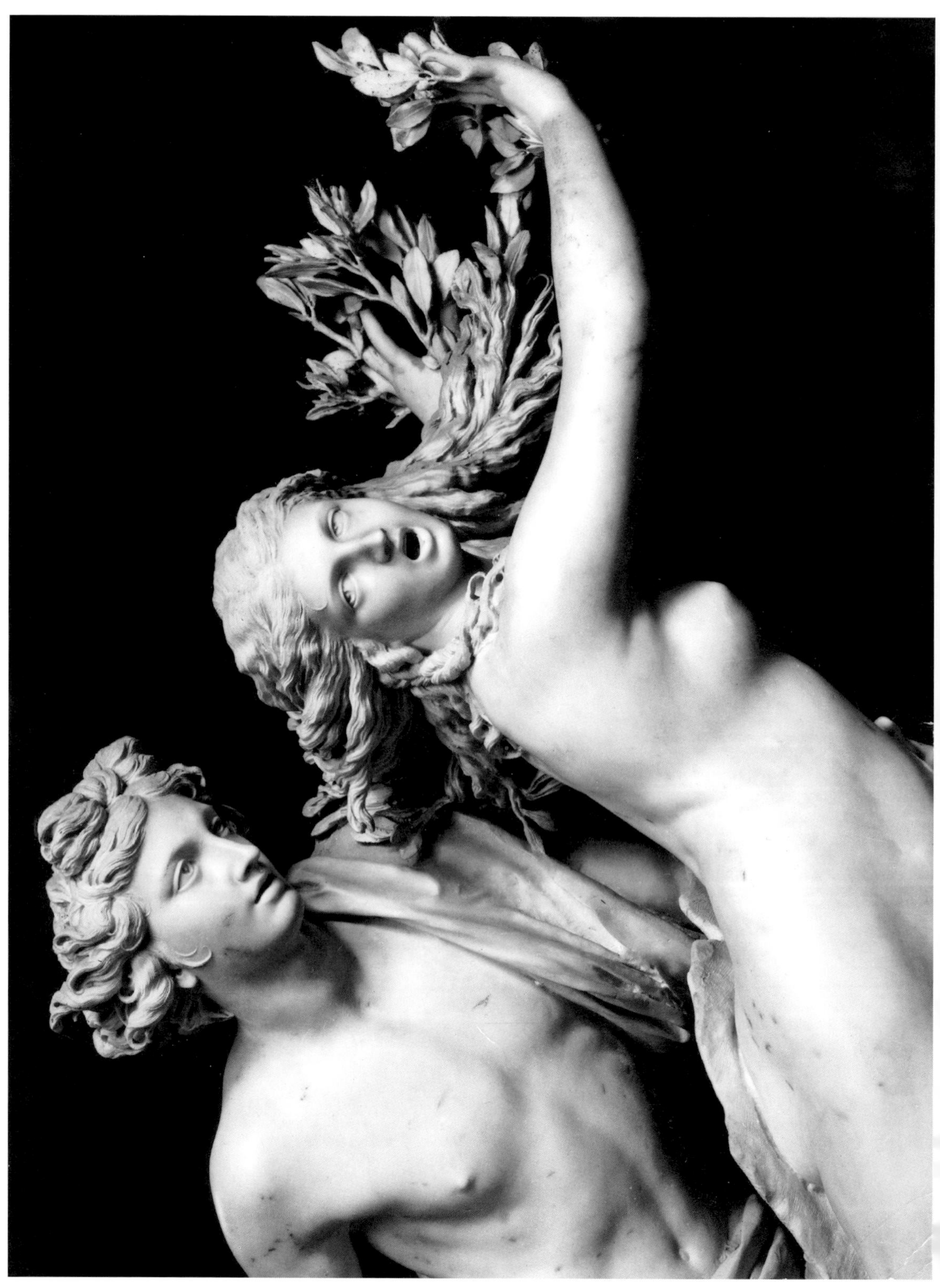

Gianlorenzo Bernini, APOLLO AND DAPHNE, detail, 1622–1625

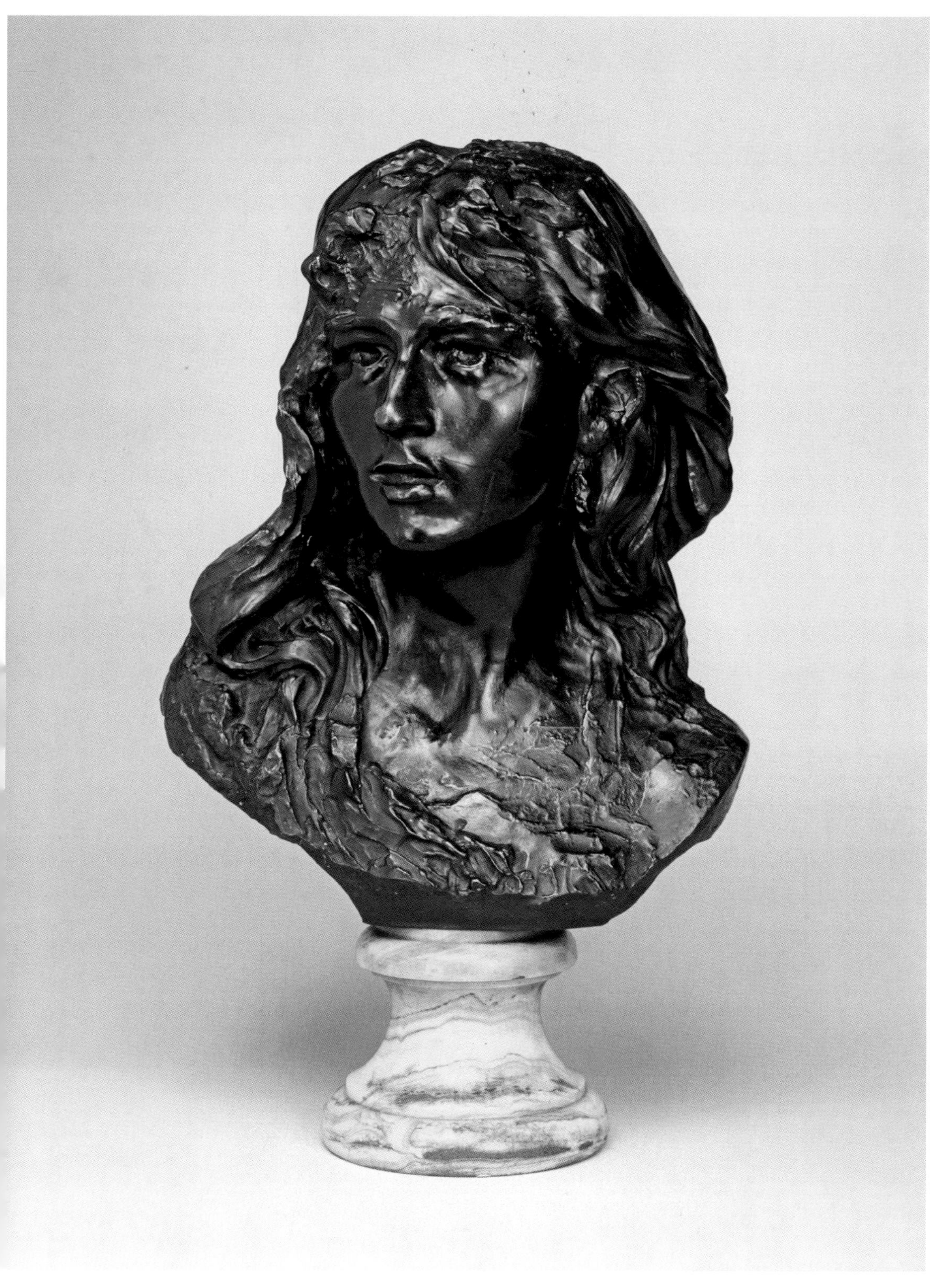

Auguste Rodin, MIGNON, 1867–1868 (cast 1925)

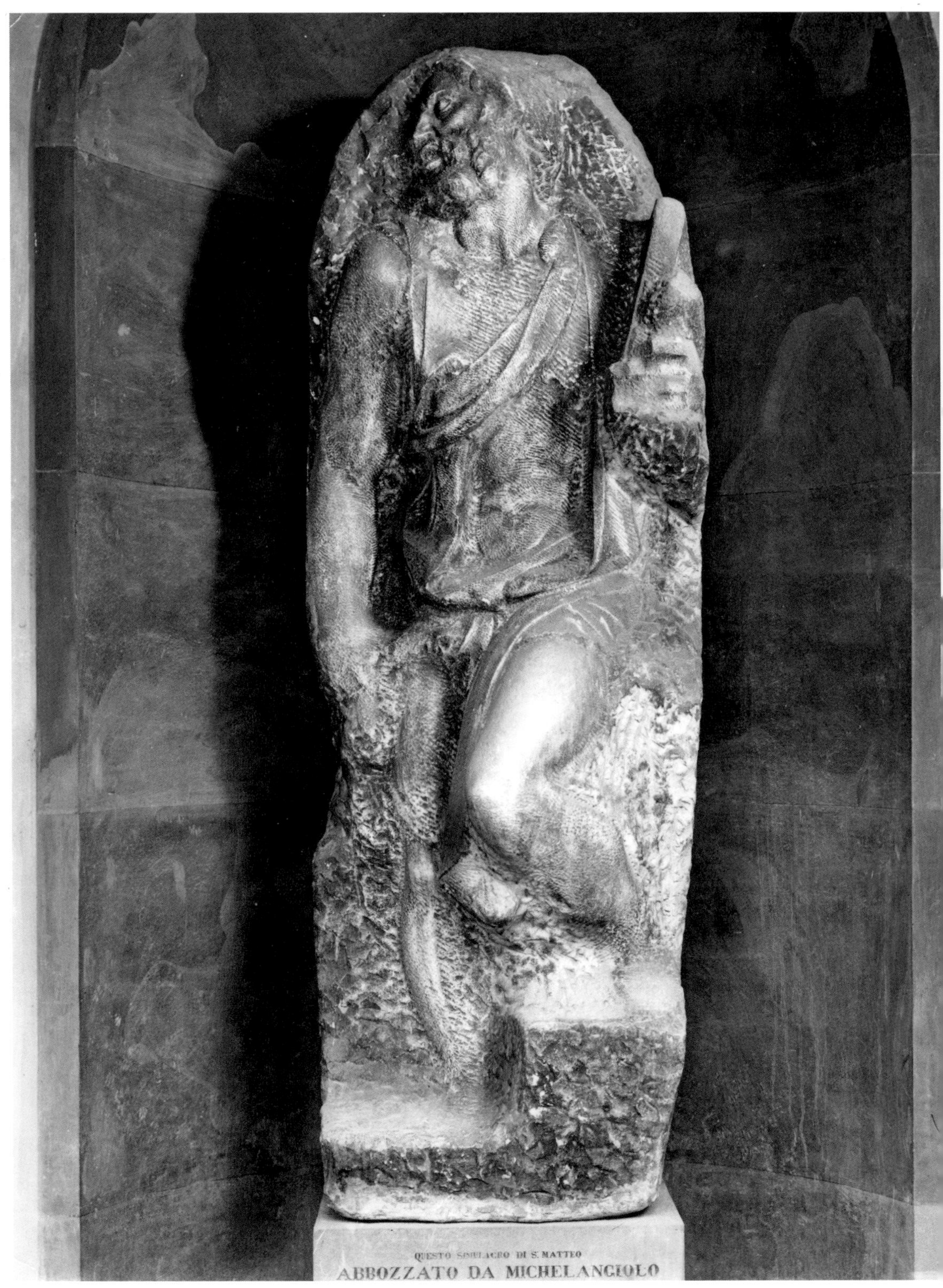


Michelangelo Buonarroti, ST. MATTHEW, ca. 1506

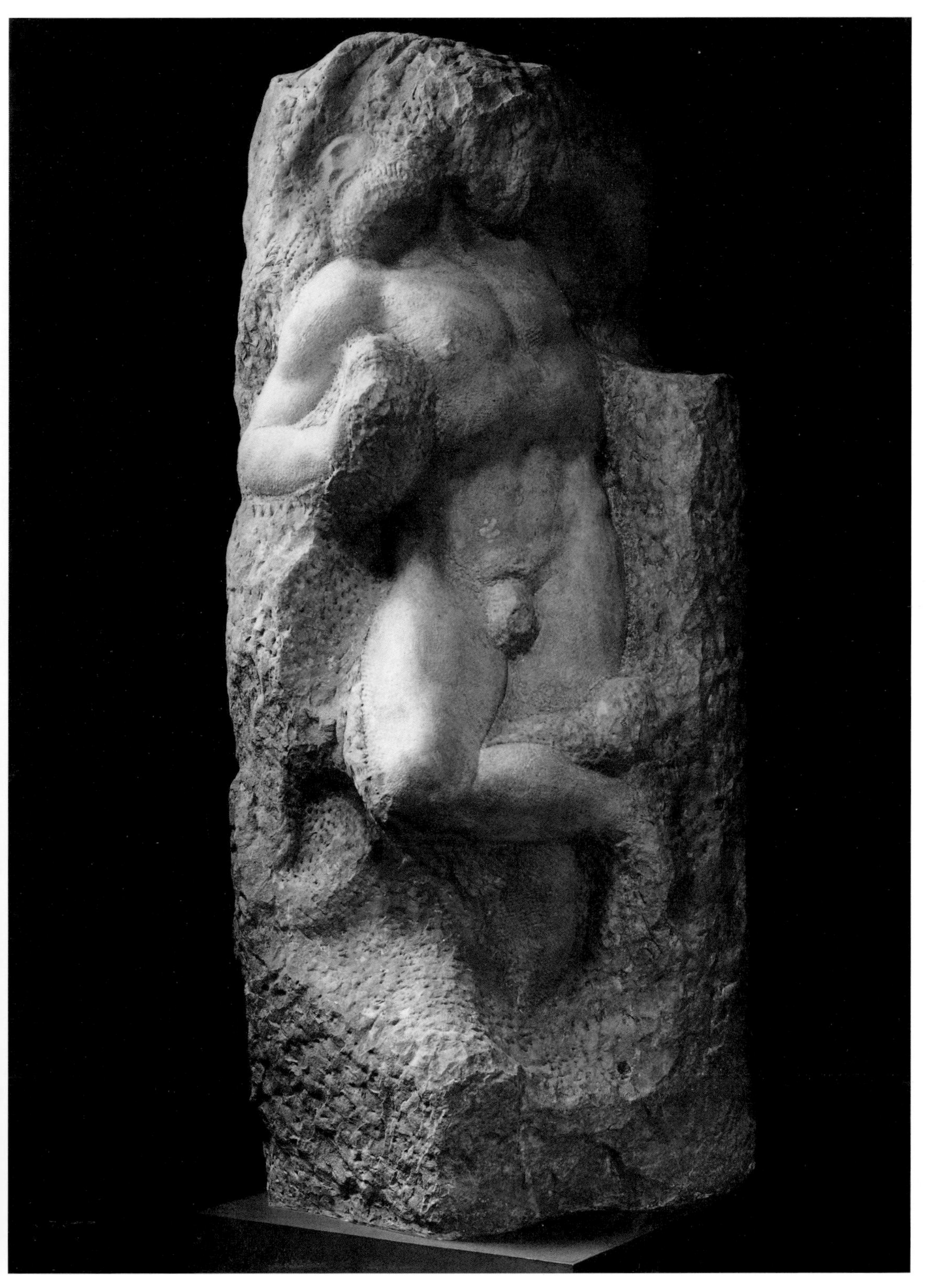

Michelangelo Buonarroti, CAPTIVE, 1519

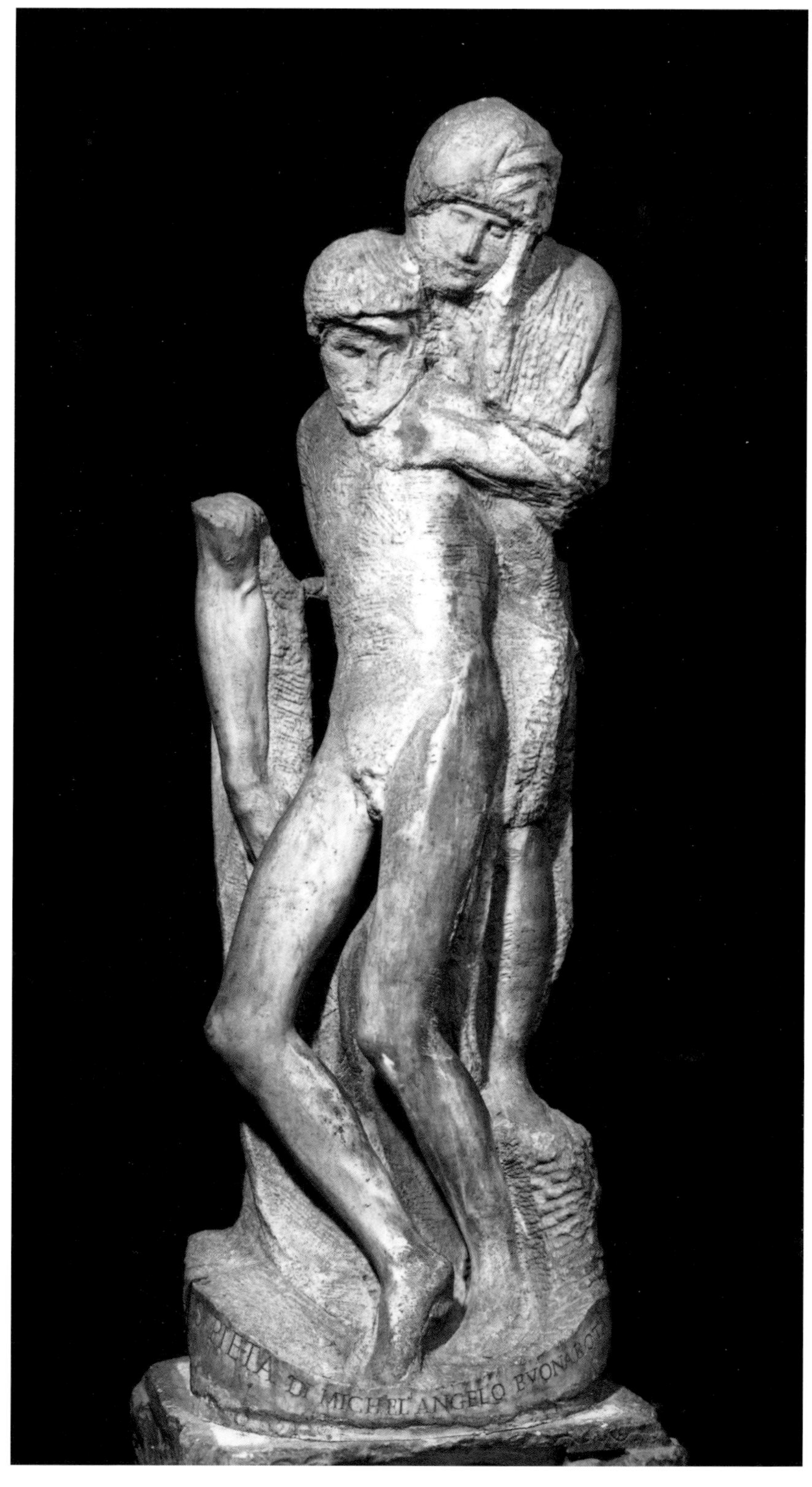


Michelangelo Buonarotti, RONDANINI PIETÀ, 1564

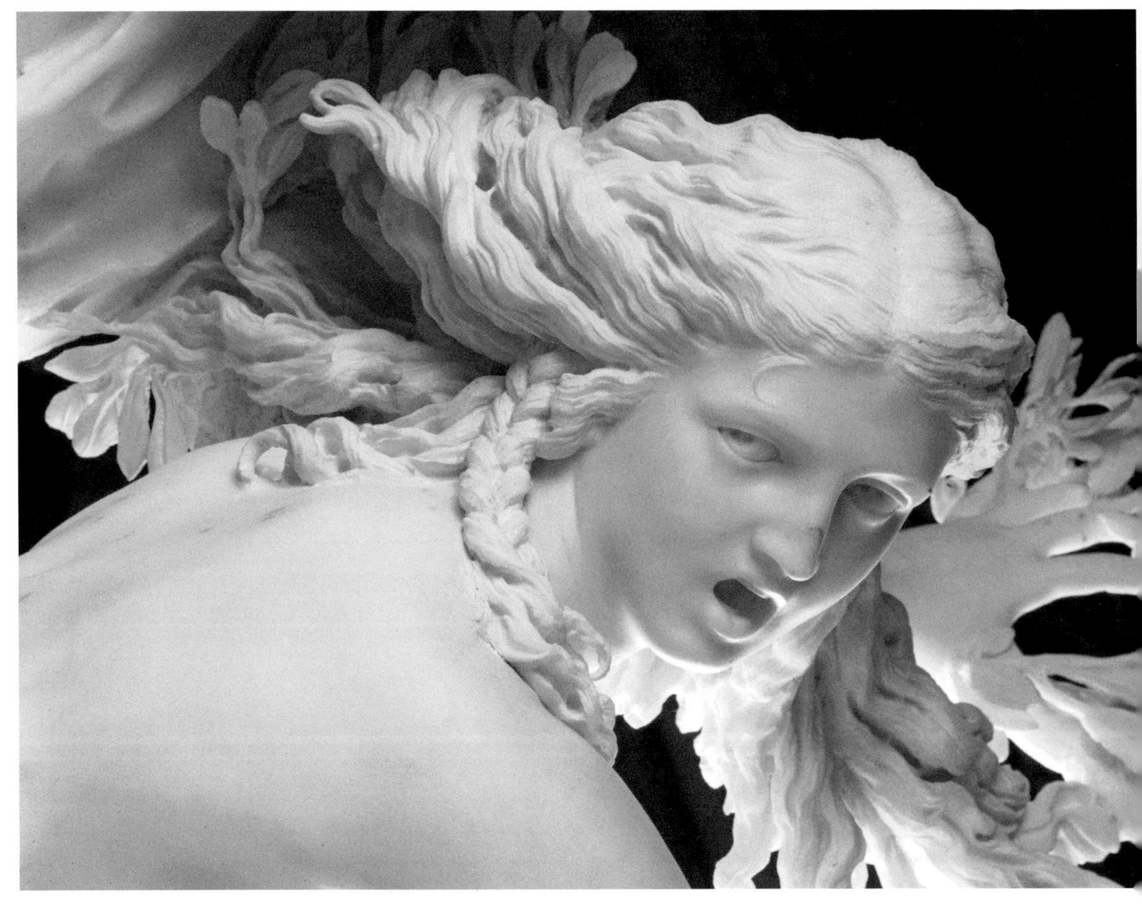

THE EXPANSIVE BAROQUE EDGE: APOLLO AND DAPHNE
*The Baroque breaks with the Classical/Renaissance containing edge to merge the object with the surrounding space. Edges are violently active; Bernini's contour conveys impermanent poses and split-second timing.*

Gianlorenzo Bernini, APOLLO AND DAPHNE (detail of Daphne's hair)

*Chapter II*

# THE BAROQUE: GIANLORENZO BERNINI

Two aspects of Baroque edges are to emerge as influences on contemporary sculpture: the edge that expands and the edge that dissolves. The quintessential Baroque artist is Gianlorenzo Bernini (1598–1680); the quintessential Baroque city is Rome. Urban VIII, pope between 1623 and 1644, aptly said, "Bernini was made for Rome and Rome was made for him."

One can say without exaggeration that Rome is dominated by Bernini's orchestration of sculptural and architectural edges.

In sculpture, the Baroque edge breaks with the earlier conception of sculpture as conforming to and reflecting a discrete block of stone and replaces it with the concept that the figure should merge with the surrounding space. The unifying rhythms of great Baroque art both connect the sculptural outlines to space and, within the outer contour, create a bravura multiplicity of diagonals, horizontals, and verticals. Bernini's sculpted male nudes in Rome's Piazza Navona look dynamic from every side. The sculptures' rhythms connect to the space of the Piazza Navona, adding a fascinating variety of horizontal and vertical lines within the flickering "boundary edge." The beholder cannot resist walking around these revolving forms, following the vortex movement of the sculpture.

Bernini saw himself as an "amico dell acqua" (friend of water), as he told his biographer Freart de Chantelou (1609–1694). Dissolving the boundaries of form and water was one of Bernini's great achievements. As the historian Simon Schama has observed:

> From the outset, Bernini had wanted to liberate the kinetic qualities of light and water from the rather stolid forms in which the fountain Sculptors of the High Renaissance had encased them. While they had Stressed the contrary properties of stone mass and running water, Bernini wanted to bring them together in one fluid, musical sequence.[1]

It is no surprise to learn that Bernini's enchantment with water penetrated all aspects of his life. He produced a play called THE FLOODING OF THE TIBER, in which he arranged for water to pour from the back of the stage towards the front rows, diverted at the last moment by a canal that was hidden from the spectators. His inventiveness with water ranged in all directions, including an ingenious device for his insomniac pope. Bernini constructed a small water-circulating machine, which was placed outside the pope's bedchamber. The repetitive sounds of gushing water from this small object evoked a mighty river or the waves of the ocean and soothed the pontiff to sleep.[2]

The most joyful and skillful examples of Bernini's tour de force of edge and edgelessness are his fountains.

Besdies dramatizing Bernini's passion for water, his FOUNTAIN OF THE FOUR RIVERS (Fontana dei Quattro Fiumi, 1648-1651, p. 81) embodies cosmic and mythological ideas. At the feet of the four river gods is a primordial world of snakes, rocks, and plants, in addition to a rearing horse and a dragon—all splashing in the churning pools below the huge figures.

Richly textured "edges" carved in the elemental playful scene—from the horse's tail to the rough texture of the rocks and the scales of the dragon—take the viewer into the drama and give authenticity to the seething animal scene. Bernini used the energy implied in the figures' extravagant gestures to locate the spatial focus of the sculptural mass outside of the statues themselves.

Primarily known for his rhythmic, active contours, Bernini was an unsurpassed original in creating surface textures. APOLLO AND DAPHNE (p. 28) is an early masterpiece—1622–1624—which shows both a flickering, dissolving outer contour and astonishing surfaces. Only nineteen years old when he carved it, Bernini chose to depict the moment when Daphne's long, sensuous hair billows over her shoulder in her attempt to repel Apollo's erotic embrace. Late in life, when carving the bust of LOUIS XIV (p. 83) in Paris, Bernini is said to have spoken with pride of Daphne's spectacularly carved hair—luxurious yet somehow gossamer—and he cited his marble carving as having created "strands of lightness." Daphne's supremely poetic hair is a perfect example of the "dissolving edge." (p. 34)

Three masterpieces of Bernini's show the artist's genius at inventing poses of compelling serpentine rhythms. In PLUTO AND PROSERPINA (1621–1622) Proserpina pushes Pluto's head away in her struggle to escape. The pose dramatizes the most intense moment in the narrative, when it seems that Pluto has finally captured his victim. The two figures are in extreme contrapposto, leaning sharply backward at the waist. Cerberus, the three-legged dog who guards the underworld, adds to the dramatic movement by urging one to circle the work. The crisp marble perimeters of Proserpina's tears are, like Pluto's eager fingers on her thigh, celebrated edges in sculpture. As in APOLLO AND DAPHNE, the hair and curls echo the curvilinear movements of the whirling bodies. The contradiction in the poses—Proserpina both leans toward Pluto and pushes him away—conveys a compelling rhythm and vitality unique to Bernini.

The viewer's excitement with a Bernini "sculpture of action" like DAVID (p. 80) has to do with split-second timing, similar to the energy tensed and released in a balletic leap of Baryshnikov. Bernini invented supremely impermanent poses, at the beginning of an action, that sudden violent micro-second before David swings the stone at Goliath, Daphne leaves her body to become a tree, or Pluto ravishes Persephone. Bernini's mastery of the pose is such that the viewer identifies the "very next moment of action" with his own body.

Bernini's use of the energy in split-second timing relates the edges of his statues to surrounding space—examples of what we have been calling the "expanding edge." His DANIEL (1655–1661) in the Chigi Chapel of the church of Santa Maria del Popolo in Rome shows the artist's creation of a stance in which the prophet's arms and legs generate a strong rhythm. As he prays for salvation, Daniel's body thrusts upward from his sharply bent knees. In triangulating Daniel's arms, Bernini devised a bravura pose that is partly derived from the LAOCOON. However, Bernini takes this motif and transforms it into a more sinuous version of Michelangelo's renowned flamelike shape—likewise influenced by LAOCOON.

Daniel's legs and the angel's arm burst out of the niche into the space of the spectator and church. The body's theatrical contour, mirrored by the drapery, creates a sophisticated play of diagonal movements. The textures reflect his skill in manipulating terracotta surfaces later to be carved in marble. (Recent X-ray fingerprint technology has proven that the ridges and projections of the clay were made by Bernini's own fingers.) Examples of textures are the lion's tongue, the silky polished marble of Daniel's skin and the hair of the angel. Daniel's cloak turns around the arm with a twirl and counter-twirl of drapery, down his torso. The work is a tour de force of contrasted energies, a contrappostal play of diagonals. A driving, rhythmic force urges every modulation delineating Daniel's body and drapery. These powerful rhythms create a heightened vitaliy, which most art writers, from Aristotle onwards, agree is a chief course of artistic pleasure. Once again, this heightened vitality is largely a result of the artist's treatment of edge.

Bernini's portraits are another example of the artist's flickering edges. Rather than wanting his subjects to sit "still" (one recalls Cézanne exhorting Madame Cézanne to be an apple), Bernini insisted that the sitter be "moving and talking." We admirers of Bernini are lucky that the artist's creation of the portrait of LOUIS XIV is recorded in great detail in the diary of Chantelou.[3] In his astonishing portrait bust of LOUIS XIV, he urged the king to move his head and shoulders from side to side while conversing.

The King and Bernini definitely did converse, according to Chantelou. Once when his eyes met that of the King, Bernini said: "I am stealing your likeness." The King responded "Yes, but only to give it back." Bernini did not hold back: he boasted to the King about making the Venetian lace of the King's shirt turn into marble.

This celebrated image of Le Roi Soleil has verve, poetry, and unity—the result of the artist's choice of pose, the turn of the head, and the rhythmic composition of the drapery. The dynamic energy of the bust lies in Bernini's inspired carving of drapery into vehement plastic volumes that pull in two directions. The king looks and turns his torso to one side, while the drapery moves violently to the other, and then, with a sudden change of tempo, the drapery becomes a vertical frame.

While not strictly sculpture, Bernini's Piazza San Pietro is what Noguchi called a "sculpting of space" in an unprecedented, grand manner.

This monumental embrace of columns, forming a vast oval, is the most visually dramatic "edge against space" in Rome, if not in the world. Under the direction of Pope Alexander VII, Bernini followed the distinguished Bramante and Michelangelo in the design of the complex of St. Peter's. After Bernini had worked five years on the interior of the Basilica, the Pope asked Bernini to design a Piazza "so that the greatest number of people could see the Pope give his blessing, either from the middle of the façade of the church or from a window in the Vatican Palace." Bernini's solution was a space far bigger than the church itself, with four columns deep of colossal Tuscan columns which created a spatial entity of unsurpassed scale. This Piazza is an example of simultaneously containing and expansive edges: the forms of church, Piazza, and colonnade are what Bernini described as the "maternal arms of Mother Church."[4] The wings Bernini created that connect St. Peter's façade to the colossal oval piazza—240 meters across—form a trapezoid that makes the Basilica seem taller.[5]

The Piazza San Pietro shows the contrast between the Renaissance building which was contained and self-sufficient and the Baroque design which relates to the outer world and surrounding space. Art historians have noted that the expansiveness of the Baroque existed in science and poetry as well as art: the new astronomy and physics of Galileo and Newton; Pascal's words "the silence of infinite spaces frightens me"; Milton's phrase "the vast and boundless deep" also expresses the Baroque image of space.

Bernini's works are triumphs of rhythmic vigor and poetic imagination. They show the Baroque at its most daring, a style which majestically flaunts its impermanence and spatial incompleteness. Modern abstract sculptors show an affinity to Bernini's patterns of movement; Maya Lin, Robert Lobe, Giuseppe Penone, and Jian Jun Zhang all make expanding and dissolving edges part of their signature styles. Between Bernini and modern times, however, another giant explored the edge: Auguste Rodin.

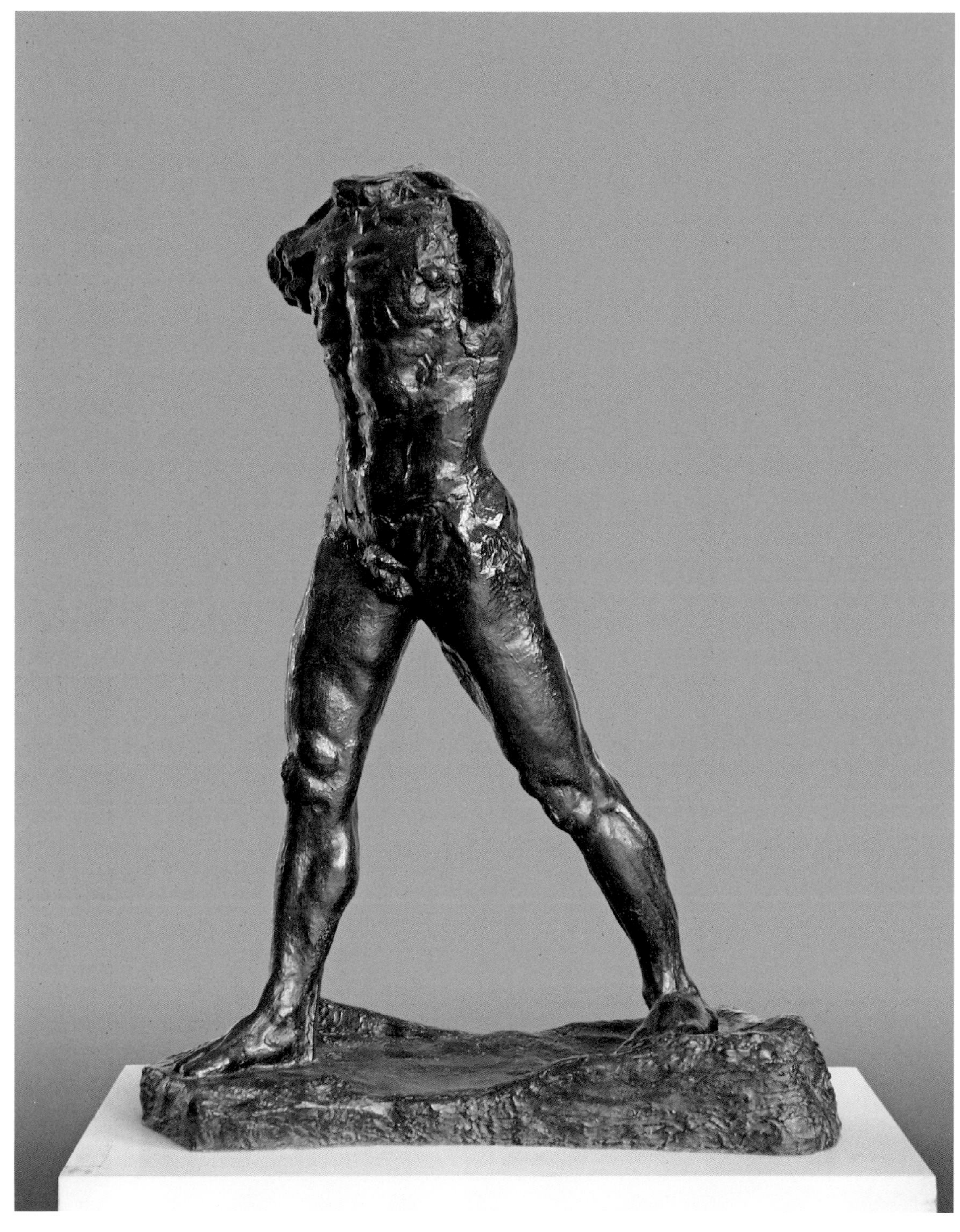

Auguste Rodin, L'HOMME QUI MARCHE, 1877–1878 (cast 1917)

## *Chapter III*

# TRANSITIONAL GIANT: AUGUSTE RODIN

In an art historical framework, Auguste Rodin (1840–1917) is the nineteenth-century artist who continues the Renaissance and Baroque vocabulary of Michelangelo and Bernini. A transitional figure, Rodin carries the old-master figurative lineage into the modern and abstract traditions. Through Rodin, we see Michelangelo's *non-finito* transferred to a great modern sculptor like Noguchi. Rodin was able to combine two kinds of edges—a complexity of multiple contours and volatile surface edges. He is a perfect example of that multiplicity and unity crucial to the aesthetic of a work of art.

To look at Rodin's bronzes such as MIGNON, 1867–1868 (p. 29), or L'HOMME QUI MARCHE, 1877 (p. 40), one is struck by both the drama of the outer contours and by the turbulent, active surfaces of the bronze.

The way we perceive these contours and surfaces is to look for more than one contour and then to take in all the surfaces. Rodin's surface edges include the infinite number of ridges and grooves that make up the variations of texture and plane in the material. Rodin created light—something he identified as his chief goal—through his gouged and worked bronze surfaces. As he put it:

> To look for form in Nature and bring out grace, vigor, amorous charm, or the untamed fire by taking form, amplifying it, exaggerating the holes and bumps so as to give them more light, after which I search for a synthesis of the whole.[1]

The expressive drama of outer contour, and the inner energy expressed through the surfaces give Rodin's work its sensuous power. The muscularity of Rodin is owed to Michelangelo, but the grandiloquence and spatial energy echoes Bernini. In their portraits of their lovers, Rodin shares with Bernini a capacity to convey an inner passion which pushes upwards to the surface. The sensuous open lips of MIGNON, Rodin's lover Rose Beuret, recalls Bernini's portrait of Constanza Buonarelli, and the mass of Beuret's windswept curls is as charismatic as Daphne's cascading strands of hair (p. 34).

Rodin came to believe that in order for a pose to be truly convincing, a figure must combine two phases of one continuous action into the pose.[2]

Rodin's uncanny knowledge of how to fuse two aspects of an action into a single pose was a result of his insistence that his many models move continually about his studio, as well as his keen and ceaseless observation of figures in Paris's streets. At the point in his life when he created IRIS (1880), Rodin was fascinated by dancers and often stopped and sketched what he called the "hoodlum girls" on the rue de Lappe.

In such late works such IRIS, Rodin's genius combines the muscle of Michelangelo and the space-awareness of Bernini. The erotic pose of IRIS, and similarly sexual works, risked offending museum directors, yet Rodin considered them central to his vision, and persisted on donating them to important museums like the Victoria and Albert. Certainly IRIS is magnificent in grace and ferocious energy. As in a Baroque sculpture, it leaps into the viewer's space: one of the dancer's legs is thrust directly forward towards the spectator, while the other leg is balanced precariously on her toe. In IRIS Rodin created a unforgettable primal image. The sculpture's meanings are fully embodied in the forms themselves, which pull the viewer into their mass and volume through the emotional modeling of the sensuous bronze surfaces. Rodin said of these works, "the sculpture of antiquity sought the logic of the human body. I see its psychology."

In Rodin's works of different periods, from MIGNON, AGE OF BRONZE (1877) to later works like IRIS, the artist expresses inner feelings by the mobility of the muscles.

The pose of Rodin's AGE OF BRONZE was inspired by Michelangelo's DYING SLAVE,[3] to which it bears a curious kinship. Rodin spoke of his crucial trip to Italy and how Michelangelo's poses differed from the antique and from what became his own perception of the body. He was influenced not only by Michelangelo's vision and achievement and by the Renaissance artist's expression of suffering. Rodin said to his friend the critic Paul Gsell that the Greek metaphor for the human body relied on four directions, and that by placing weight on one leg, balance was sustained by counterpoise, like the movement of an accordion. Rodin then said to Gsell that Michelangelo's treatment of the body was more pessimistic. He continued:

> This shape results in very deep shadows in the hollow of the chest and under the leg. . . . We notice that his sculpture expresses the painful withdrawal of the being into himself, restless energy . . .[4]

In his AGE OF BRONZE Rodin portrayed every facet of the model's body, not just from the usual viewpoints, but also from an aerial view looking downwards, and from the point of view of one crouched below the figure, looking up. Rodin said:

> I first look at the front, the back, and the two profiles. Then I do the intermediates, which means three-quarter profiles. And then I do it again, producing profiles that are tighter and tighter, cleaning them up, since the human body has an infinite number of profiles, I do as many as I can, and need to.[5]

In L'HOMME QUI MARCHE, one sees Rodin's genius at creating changing, multiple silhouettes and also in expressing inner emotions through the ripple and torsion of musculature. Here the figure somehow expresses two "voices," the active and the passive. The left leg forcefully twists backward in a dynamic stride, while the torso is passive and still. It is a brilliant pose, partly because, like Bernini's DAVID (p. 80), Rodin's L'HOMME QUI MARCHE is realized in the middle of an action. Because of the muscles' torsion, and the seething, volatile holes and projections in the bronze surface, a single calm contour is impossible to find. Henry Moore considered L'HOMME QUI MARCHE one of the world's great sculptures and described its "feeling of hardness and softness, of a surface both rough and smooth, of depressions and expansive, of hollows and swellings."[6]

In his late years, Rodin was fascinated by the varying silhouettes of Cambodian dancers he encountered in Paris in 1906. With characteristic passion, he followed the dancers to Marseilles, where he sketched his favorites, Sap, Soun, and Yem. Rodin observed:

> These eternally beautiful human expressions both justify and heighten the artist's profound belief in the unity of nature . . . Indeed, these dances are religious because they are artistic; the rhythm is a rite, and it is the purity of the rite which ensures the purity of the rhythm.[7]

Rodin's sensitivity to surface is recorded by his famous student Malvina Hoffman, who wrote about visiting the Louvre with her teacher:

> To teach me what surfaces and planes could do Rodin would take me to the Louvre late in the day, just before closing time, and standing in silent admiration before the great Egyptian statues or the Venus de Milo would pull a candle out of his pocket, light it, and hold it up so that its light fell on the smooth, strong planes of the statues.[8]

For inventing a dramatic surface that symbolizes an inner world, Rodin has no equal, nor in his fusion of kinetic and psychological knowledge. In contrast to those of classical sculpture, Michelangelo, and the Baroque, what do the contours and edges of Rodin express? Certainly they conjure an excessive energy and a passionate spirit that stirs from deep within the body to be reenacted on the surface. One sees this kind of tactile energy and tumult again in Robert Lobe's work. Rodin's genius at making light play over the irregularities of the bronze surface projects introspection and a mood of poetic reverie. Finally, this great nineteenth-century artist fuses Michelangelo's *non-finito* with his own complex and indeterminate contours to presage the roughly chiseled edges in the great modernist Isamu Noguchi.

Rodin confirms this book's thesis that the sculpture's edge creates aesthetic beauty. Surface edges express energy both within and without the work of art; the infinite number of ridges and projections express that "incompleteness" Schapiro notes is common to great works of art.

Rodin wanted children to play on top of the BURGHERS OF

CALAIS, so that the patina of the bronze result from daily handling and interaction. It is difficult to express in words the viewer's physical and cognitive response to the meaning of edge and space. Rodin's intellect and poetic sensibility to light and shadow are beautifully expressed in his words: "To model shadows is to create thoughts."

*Chapter IV*

# FUTURISM: UMBERTO BOCCIONI

The gestalt of Boccioni is fervently classical modernist, in that modernist mode of urgent idealism that art could and should change the world. Bernini and Boccioni's sculptures both express compelling images of movement and change. Boccioni's figures become part of the surrounding space just as Bernini's become fused with space; however the images of change and spatial movement have radically different intellectual contexts and subject matter. Bernini was inspired by fiercely mystical religious beliefs and wanted his sculptures to express aspiration to union with God. Boccioni, by contrast, conceived of a totally secular context of belief.

One of the most overwhelmingly inventive sculptures, UNIQUE FORMS OF CONTINUITY IN SPACE (p. 84) shows Boccioni incorporating all three kinds of edges in his art: containing, expanding, and in flux. The speeding, lunging figure is only literally "contained" by the zigzagging outer contour, while the figure's seething muscular volumes "expand" and refuse to be contained. Inside the outer boundaries, forms like the individual muscles in arms and thighs are fragmented into units of perpetual kinesis.

Boccioni succeeds in showing how the units of the body, as muscles and sinews, struggle together to create an action. He does this by using a spiraling centrifugal architecture. With the exception of Noguchi, who consciously adapted theories of Japanese aesthetics about edge, most artists in this book are not theoretic about contours. By contrast, the Futurists went zealous over theories, about Futurist clothes, Futurist cuisine, and even theoretical exhortations to nightclub singers to dye their hair green and their breasts blue. Boccioni, in a way that Abakanowicz and Lin would echo later, had a passionate belief that the sculptural edge should encompass and pull into itself the space beyond—in this case, the wild activity of the street.[1]

Futurism started in 1909 as a riotous avant-garde poetry rebellion headed by the movement's high priest, Filippo Tommaso Marinetti. In the beginning, the now famous manifestos were led off with a bang on February 20, 1909, when the newspaper *Le Fi-*

*garo* published the first, impassioned, solely literary manifesto. The second Futurist manifesto, *The Manifesto of Futurist Painting*, of 1911, was signed by various painters and sculptors, all of whom are now lavishly represented by masterpieces in New York's Museum of Modern Art, namely: Umberto Boccioni, Giacomo Balla, Gino Severini, Carlo Carrà, Luigi Russolo, and Gino Severini.

The manifestos proclaimed an ardent rejection of the past and all the cultural institutions that served the past; they exhorted artists and the public to exalt power, to embrace the present with its violence, machines, and speed, and to welcome all technology and the industrial world: "We declare that all subjects previously used must be swept aside in order to express our whirling life of steel, of pride, of fever, and of speed." "We will destroy the museums, libraries, academies of every kind. We establish Futurism because we want to free this land from its smelly gangrene of professors, archeologists, and antiquarians." Indeed, Futurism had a feverish tone.

The two geniuses of the group were Umberto Boccioni and Giacomo Balla. It was clear that the central idea to Futurist art was a belief in a "universal dynamism." This vision brought together the intuitive aesthetic of Henri Bergson and the vitalist philosophy of Friedrich Nietzsche, as well as the precursors of contemporary science. Bergson's books, particularly *Matter* and *Memory*, 1911, were translated into Italian and of great importance to the Futurists, and particularly to Boccioni. Boccioni's great achievement was to make permanent the Bergsonian and Futurist principle of flux. This was pungently expressed in the manifestos of 1911 and 1912:

> No one can any longer believe that an object ends where there are definite lines and closed sculpture. We break open the figure and enclose it in the environment.[2]
> The gesture which we could reproduce on canvas shall no longer be a fixed moment in universal dynamism. It should simply be the dynamic sensation itself. Indeed, all things move, all things run, all things are rapidly changing.[3]

Boccioni's great sculptures, for example, UNIQUE FORMS

OF CONTINUITY IN SPACE, all to a degree embody precisely the Futurist goal: breaking open the figure and enclosing it in the environment: the running human figure in the former, and the gyrating bottle in the latter, succeed in conjuring the sense of an object which hurls itself violently through space.

In his essay of 1914, "What Divides Us from Cubism," Boccioni focuses on the issue of dramatic action, declaring disparagingly that the Cubists were only analyzers of "fixity, who killed unity, fervor, and emotion in art by isolating the object and suppressing movement." By contrast to Cubism, Boccioni affirms the greatness of Futurism in creating an ever-accelerating narrative of motion—of the gravitation, displacement, reciprocal attraction of forms, masses, and colors.

Both in paintings and sculptures, Boccioni used what he called "lines of force," which he saw as inscribing the unimpeded internal dynamic of forms. Many distrust the exaggerated rhetoric of Futurism, thinking it to be empty speechifying; the works, however, speak for themselves. Futurist forms, wrote Boccioni, have a life outside of intelligence, since they expand beyond the limited faculties of empirical analysis and project themselves into the infinite.

The metaphysical principles of Futurism were extremely influential on subsequent artists such as Paul Klee. Klee's words echo Futurism's ardent idealism about metaphysics:

> A certain fire, an impulse to create, is kindled, is transmitted through the hand, leaps to the canvas, and in the form of a spark leaps back to its starting place, completing the circle—back to the eye and further back (back to the source of the movement, the will, the idea). The pictorial work was born of movement, is itself recorded movement, and is assimilated through movement (eye muscles).[4]

Lucio Fontana is the most brilliant and original modernist heir to Boccioni. Fontana proudly expressed his great debt to Futurism. Fontana's CONCETTI SPAZIALI are elegant and mysterious paintings that recall Futurism's kinetic patterns. The delicate perforations and tiny encrustations which occur on these canvas surfaces are certainly sculptural "changes," sometimes in the form of textured beams of light, and sometimes more like scattered beads, jewels, or stones. By his evocation of a definite space, like an ellipse, and then his departure from that shape, Fontana's nocturnal works of Venice simultaneously evoke the spatial grandeur of St. Mark's Square and the infinite space of the night sky.

Contemporary sculptors like Tony Cragg, while they do not cite Futurist influences, certainly reference Futurist forms and evoke the Futurist theme of perpetual kinesis. And one only need to look at the skyline of major cities to see in Zaha Hadid and Frank Gehry boundaries in expansion and constant flux. Today's architecture uses computers and industrial materials with a flamboyant panache that would have pleased Boccioni.

If Noguchi represents the edge internalized, then Boccioni represents the edge aggressively externalized.

*Chapter V*

# ISAMU NOGUCHI

In Noguchi, one sees the link between the life-giving energy of the *non-finito*/incompleteness and the Zen aesthetic about imperfection. Noguchi's treatment of edge and space was inspired by the ancient world as well as by his own poetic and philosophical mind. Noguchi's basically Japanese vision of stone as ceremonial is a consistent theme in his work. His austere yet voluptuous drama of edge and surface symbolizes continuity and the infinite, and links man to a universe of *mujo* and *seisruten*, or mobility and constant change. Edges in Noguchi occur from the way he alternates raw, unperfected marble or stone with the intercessions of art, often inspired by the sensuous, richly textured surfaces and irregular shapes of Raku tea bowls, or the raked sand gardens of Tokyo temple gardens. Noguchi, as he himself said, considered himself fortunate to have been born near the sea, in Japan, where he was profoundly inspired by the primal force of water. All inspired Noguchi, in his own words, to retain the ancient link to nature by going "beyond geometry to the metaphysics of nature." Of the artists discussed in this book, Noguchi most and best used the expressive edge. He not only exploited the edge's formal and aesthetic potential, but again and again embodied in his art the intense poetic and philosophical nuances of the Japanese concept *hashi*. Noguchi called this "the limit of one world, assuming the existence of another world beyond . . . anything that crossed, filled, or projected into the chasm of MA, space between two edges." Indeed, part of the meaning of *hashi* as edge was behind Noguchi's profound belief in art's function to move beyond a given sculpture's finite edge into life itself. "Art has to do with people's places in the world, their sense of belonging," he said in 1979. "I think that kind of thing can be suggested by art."[1]

Even in Noguchi's most geometric and Western public works, like the Beinecke sunken courtyard at Yale, or THE BLACK SUN (p. 105) in Seattle, an Eastern sensibility prevails, and the work takes on a character that is mythical. While the forms themselves are Euclidean, the intense mood they create is that of meditative objects in a strange, almost Symbolist tableau. In the Chase Manhattan Plaza, seven rocks, which the artist "dragged out of the bottom of the Uji River," activate the space with no dead or empty space between them. The spatial rhythm is Noguchi's, but it recalls the famous rhythm between space-attracting entities of the Ruoyan-ji Garden in Kyoto.[2]

Noguchi, committed to a kinetic, natural universe and to larger definition of the function of sculpture in the world, was able to imbue material itself with the drama of the act of creation. In VERTICAL VIEW (p. 85) the broken edge or contour, like Cézanne's repeated arcs of dark blue lines, relates the sculptures to nature and to surrounding space.

In his work, Noguchi clearly explored a number of linked issues: Western and Eastern ideas about geometry, for example, and horizontal and vertical space. He also pondered the Eastern values of asymmetry and imperfection, and the notion, originally derived from Shinto, that nature—and specifically stone—was inhabited by living spirits. Finally, he was fascinated by a sense of kinesis that arises from images of external movement; this dovetailed with his own belief in a tactile life within inorganic matter.

Many of his most beautiful works, like those of Bernini before him and Maya Lin after him, use water, and the flow of water, as subject matter. For example, in the breathtaking interior garden/fountain Noguchi made for the Sogetsu Kaikan, in 1977–1978, and again in 1983 for the DOMON KEN MUSEUM GARDEN in Sakata, Japan, Nougchi made the water flow over the entire area of granite steps and cascade into the lake. In WATER STONE, 1987, Noguchi creates a water basin out of basalt, in a mood that recalls the quiet mood of stone basins in Japanese garden. However, in a manner echoed some thirty years later by Maya Lin, Noguchi, rather than having the water fall down into the basin/well from above, created a way for the water to flow up from the ground—the earth covered with a bed of white rocks—then over the rim into the basin. The artist saw water as a natural creator of sculpture as well as a material of sculpture, like rocks which had been eroded into beautiful ragged-edged forms.

Noguchi sees and treats landscape, and its molecular essence, stone, as metaphoric of man's being, his belonging to the earth. His later works are richer than his earlier in symbolic references to natural phenomena.

These late works, including THE BLACK SUN, LANDSCAPE

SCULPTURE (p. 23), and KNIFE IN THE ROCK, are Noguchi's most elegant studies in emerging form. They show a heightened intensity derived from the metaphor of stone itself, and what the artist saw as energies within matter. He wrote:

> I try to create forms which have relevance to outer truth and space and to inner truth. We see the exterior of the tree and inwardly we see the sap rising. The forms I try to create are not merely the appearance but the resonating energy inside.[3]

Western in its unity, Noguchi's work between 1960 and 1980 shows an Eastern sensibility, seen above all in the sculptor's determination to give the working of stone a spiritual meaning in rough, irregular surfaces and silhouettes.

By the time Noguchi had created his later works, his aesthetic had subtly changed, becoming more closely tied to Eastern ideas of imperfection and asymmetry—nature's own attributes—which we link with continuity and growth. Emerging upwards from horizontal surfaces that symbolize sea and land, or pushing down into the earth, the landscape sculptures show Noguchi creating edges and contours with an extreme both of emotional content and style. These are his most explicitly elegant works. They also express most deeply his vision of nature's dialectic with art. While the edges are jagged—chunks cut out of raw matter—the planar forms are created with great technical refinement.

The circle is a recurrent form in Noguchi's work, an example of an image central to both Western and Eastern cultures. THE RING, THE BLACK SUN, THE SUN AT NOON, and MAGIC RING each refer to different cultural meanings of the form. In ancient Chinese sculpture, the form symbolized the cosmos. THE BLACK SUN, in its mood and blackness, also shows an affinity to the bold black circle in Zen calligraphy. In Zen painting, the *enso*, or circle, is a symbol indicating an encompassing of the universe with one eternal and endless line, the Absolute Void, the continuous journey of the soul.

Noguchi was also conscious of other meanings of the circle,

which he discussed in regard to the white circle at Yale, for example, a "coiled magnet, the circle of ever-accelerating force." Irregular and imperfect in topological volumes, yet roughly circular in its linear boundaries, THE BLACK SUN expresses a dense and contained energy, and simultaneously, a form of infinite extension, without beginning or end.

THE BLACK SUN, commissioned for Seattle, was one of the many models Noguchi made for the white marble disk at Yale. Although THE BLACK SUN appears to be a perfect circle, it is subtly asymmetrical. The form's central aperture is placed left of center, for instance, and this inner circle is further distorted by the planes and ridges of the powerful plastic modeling.

THE BLACK SUN is restless and dynamic, its circularities expressing nature in a robust and almost savage mood. In contrast, the white marble disk at Yale is serene and rational. Noguchi often said that he saw art as part of a constantly mobile cosmos, and THE BLACK SUN is a powerful expression of that forever changing environment. Within its apparently fixed and familiar circular form—as in the white disk at Yale—there edges and planes create irregular movement and make the sculpture part of asymmetrical flux. The modeled forms seem to push from left to right, creating an illusion that the huge disk is rotating. Placed in a vertical position, it is conceived of plastically with a sensuously abstracted, horizontal typography. Noguchi contrasts undulating, sinuous volumes with hard-edged shapes that have flattened surfaces. In its changing rhythms of concavities and convexities, THE BLACK SUN's topography relates to Noguchi's landscape table sculptures such as KNIFE IN THE ROCK.

The landscape table sculptures of the 1970s and 1980s are perhaps the most elegant examples of Noguchi's skill at evoking the theme of emerging form through subtle edge and plane. Mainly of black granite, these works convey a form's gradual and potent growth of movement in transformation. They show the most intense contrast between aesthetic refinement and the visible, palpable process of creation, between highly worked surfaces and slabs' jagged edges. The technique of scoring, carving and pointing the stone with myriad granular markings of different sizes and depths also creates the illusion of dramatic lighting. A low-placed slab of black granite broken by a curved diagonal volume, KNIFE IN THE ROCK, in the angle of the curve and sense of suddenly arrested motion, evokes the rapid stroke of a Samurai sword.

Like the Beinecke Garden at Yale and THE BLACK SUN, the landscape tables are complex unities of Eastern and Western ideas about art and nature, horizontal and vertical, time and space. Noguchi lived by the sea in Japan until the age of thirteen and these works evoke the sense of light playing and reflecting off the sea—the drama of moonlight on water. Noguchi saw movement in these works as something not only visible but as a motion within the material:

> It's not motion going anywhere but motion of a different sort. Inside matter there are atoms constantly in motion; if we could hear this action, we would probably hear a continuous sound, a roar created by mutual communication inside matter. What I wanted was that resonating energy inside.[4]

Because of Noguchi's facility of style and superb craftsmanship, often the precise ideas in his work have been overlooked, as has the fact that his themes are inherent in his handling of materials. He has shown a consistency over the years in creating visual metaphors for philosophical and social ideas, from studies in gravity, time and space as symbols for man's destiny on earth, to monumental meditations on geometry and its opposites.

Noguchi often said, "I'm suspicious of the whole idea of styles." There is more than a bit of irony in this statement. Through nuances of edge and plane, his distinctive style lies, more than anything, in his power to imbue stone with a sense of immanent form.

His work is unique for its heroic scope, emotional presence, and use and transcendence of materials. His boldness in taking ideas and techniques to extremes of elegance and power makes his abstract forms resonate with the dynamic of life.

Noguchi not only exploited the edge's formal and aesthetic potential, but again and again embodied in his art the intense poetic and philosophical nuances of the Japanese concept *hashi*—"the limit of one world, assuming the existence of another world beyond . . . anything that crossed, filled, or projected into the chasm of MA, space between two edges." Indeed part of the meaning of *hashi* as edge was behind Noguchi's profound belief in art's function to move beyond a given sculpture's finite edge into life itself.[5]

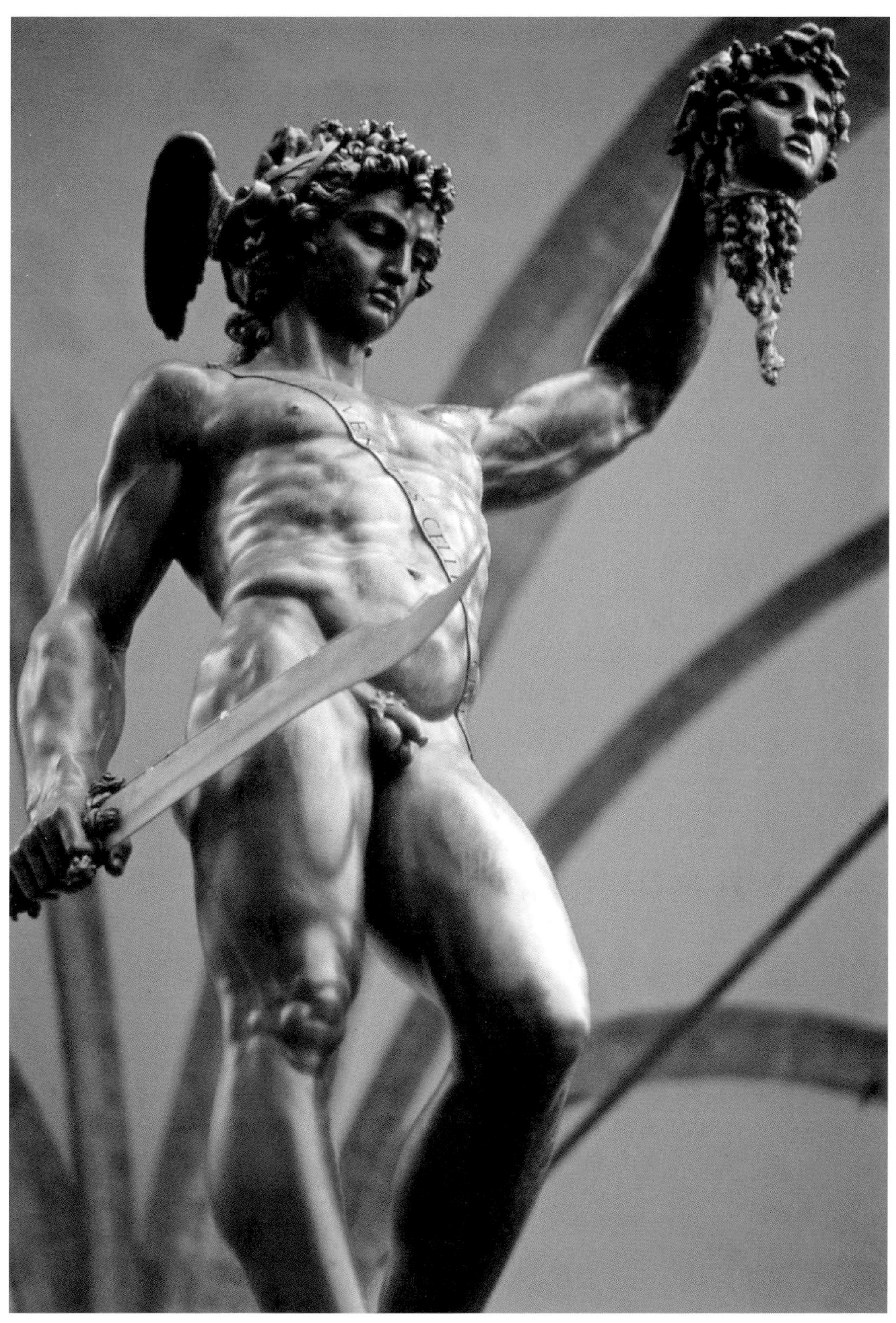

Benvenuto Cellini, PERSEUS, 1545–1553

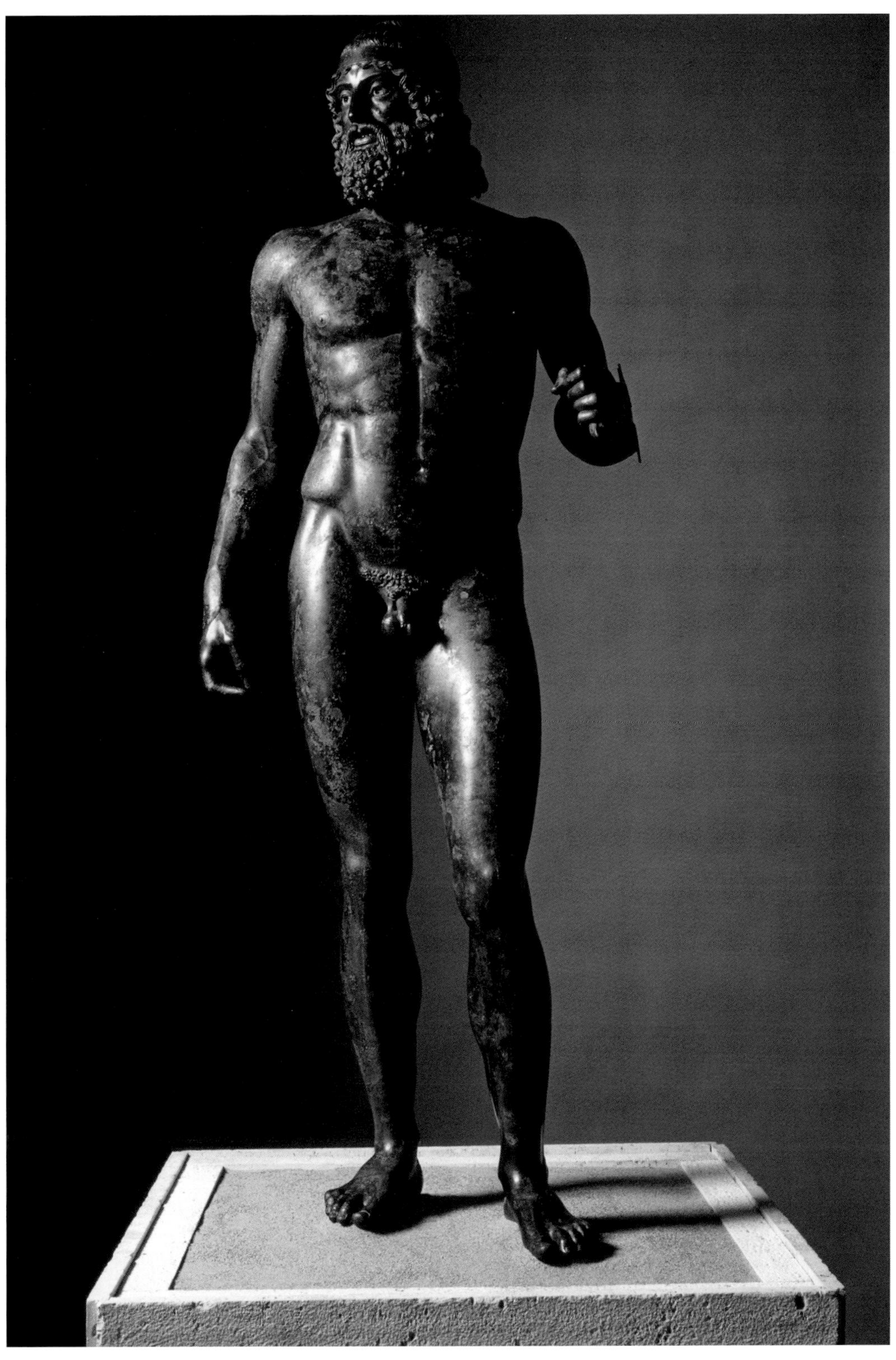

Phidias, RIACE WARRIOR (A), ca. 460 BCE

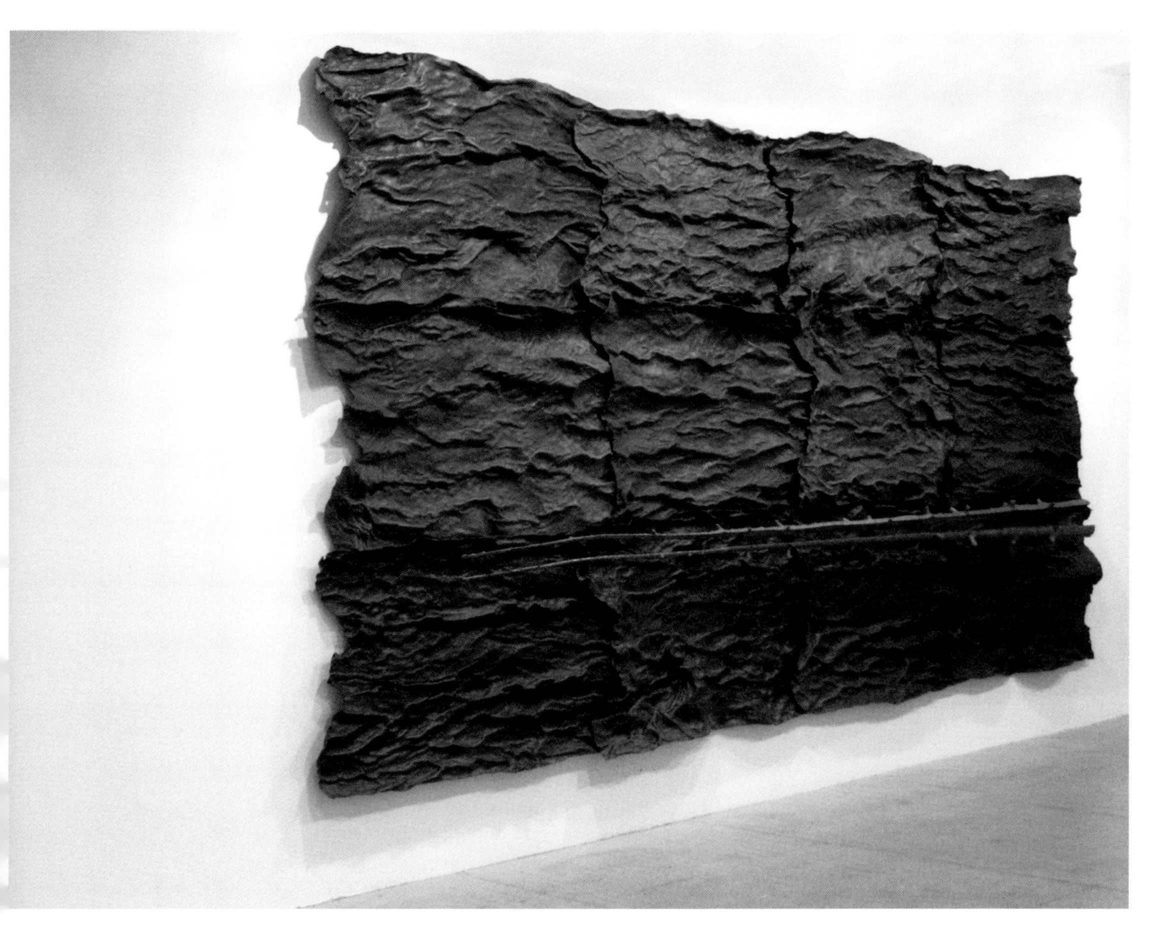

Giuseppe Penone, SCRIGNO, 2007

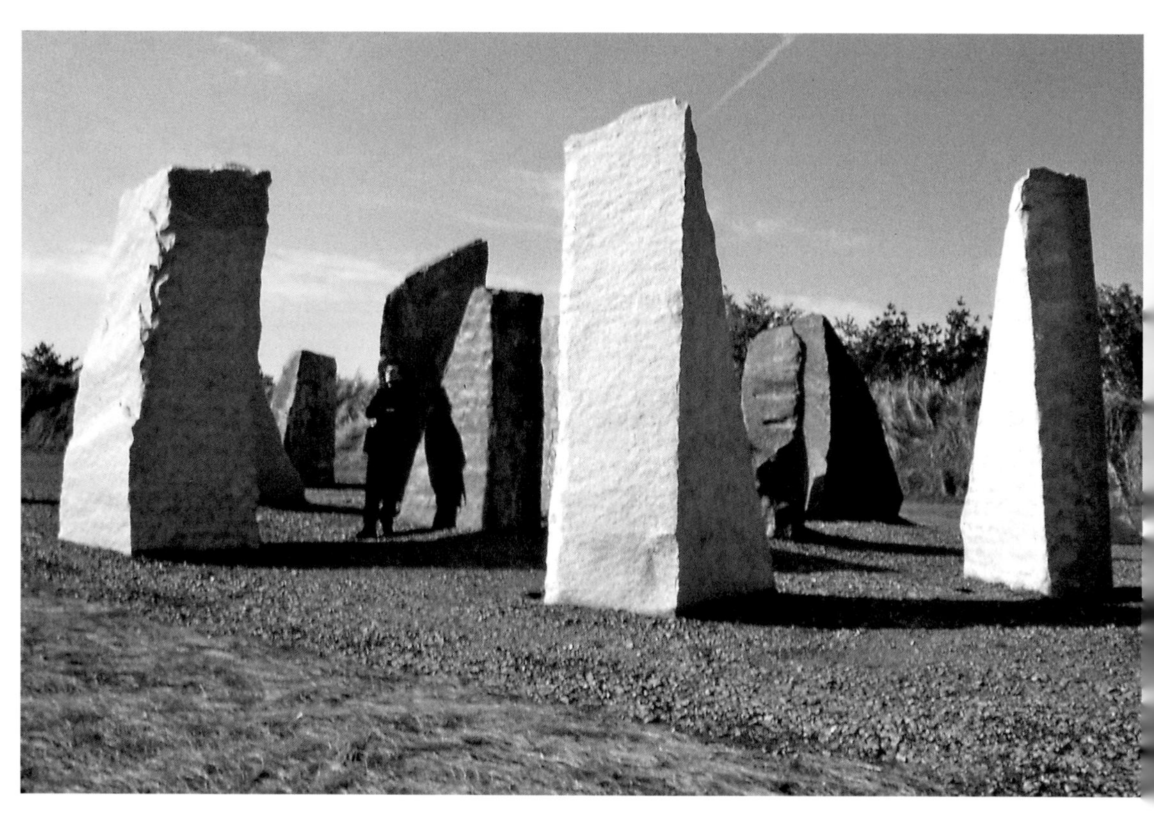

Magdalena Abakanowicz, SPACE OF STONE, 2002

*Chapter VI*

# MAGDALENA ABAKANOWICZ

Each artist's sculptural edge reflects a signature style and vocabulary. In Abakanowicz, the contours' interaction with the environmental space expresses her particular view of sculpture: "not as an object to be looked at but as a space to contemplate."[1] This effect is intensified by the artist's celebrated textures, irregular surfaces that she creates by fusing dirt, lime, and earth. Sensuous textures pull us in, making the work read as raw and damaged, with a visceral as well as intellectual power. Born in 1930 in Poland, the artist has spoken of World War II as a brutal interruption of her life. Her vocabulary of dark, mutilated figures grouped together in patterns suggesting imprisonment or slavery are stark reminders of war; these images also suggest man's self- mutilation by following the crowd.[2] Simultaneously they represent mythical ancestors. For example, works like NEGEV, 1987 (p. 101) in the Israel Museum in Jerusalem evoke ancient ceremonial sites such as Stonehenge. More recent works, like AGORA (2005)—made of one hundred cast iron figures—take up the same theme as NEGEV—the brutal, horrific loss of identity, but in a less abstract way. These two works span twenty years. NEGEV is carved out of massive disks of Jerusalem stone, is abstract, and composed of five units, and AGORA is made of cast iron, is figurative, and comprises one hundred headless figures walking in frozen movement. Radically different, they nonetheless brilliantly dramatize the artist's vision of the de-humanization and brutalization of man.

Abakaoniwicz sees sculpture as a metaphor to express what happens in the relationship of man and nature—a relationship that, as she says, "words cannot express."[3]

Abakanowicz's vision shows a palpable sense of nature's cellular energy, which recalls Noguchi's vision of stone as a universal language. She was influenced by myth, particularly by the writings of Mircea Eliade. According to Eliade, myth gives art a universal range, transcending history and politics. Thus, for Abakanowicz, Eliade was a catalyst. She responded to a question about her work, BACKS, shown at the Venice Biennale of 1980:

> When I showed BACKS in 1980, I was asked, 'Is this a concentration camp in Auschwitz or is it the dance of Ramayama

in Bali? Or it is the ritual ceremony in Peru?'
And I could answer all of these questions 'yes' because it is all of these.[4]

After a trip to Australia and Papua New Guinea, where she witnessed the tattooing and scarring of human skin, Abakanowicz simulated scarred edges in her work. The resultant marked skins of her burlap and bronze crowds had a primitivizing aura, related both to the marking of human skin and the ritual groupings of people, as well as her wartime experiences of crowds.

For KATARSIS, 1985 (p. 100), a grouping of thirty-three bronze figures in Celle, Giuliano Gori's sculpture garden in Pistoia, the artist deliberately chose "environmental" boundaries that were isolated, on stony ground, far away from the beautifully landscaped areas where the other sculptures in Gori's park were installed. The artist has said: "Katarsis could only have come into being in Celle." Art patron Gori had seen BACKS at the Venice Biennale in 1980, and asked the artist to repeat the installation for the indoor museum. As Barbara Rose accounts:

> When she finally came to the Villa Celle five years later, she was bitterly disappointed. Walking through the grounds of the romantic park filled with modern sculpture, she felt art had been trivialized; forced into the same decorative role as waterfalls, flower beds, and tailored hedges.[5]

In a rebellious state of mind, the artist chose an unlandscaped area outside the sculpture park, and surrounded by barbed wire, an unglamorous site Gori would never have intended to use. To try to convince her patron, Abakanowicz made a model of a sample figure. Finally, Gori not only accepted the project but was enthusiastic about it, and even applauded the artist's choice of bronze. Abakanowicz had decided on thirty-three figures, each 8 1/2 feet high, with the appearance of having been sliced open, so on one side one sees an empty shell. As Barbara Rose describes the figures:

> She began by carving each full-size figure out of Styrofoam blocks with a heavy kitchen knife. Then, at the foundry, a mold was made of the interior with its skeletal structure, and this, with the first mold, was used to cast the figures in bronze.[6]

It is important that the artist chose the Greek word *katarsis* for this powerful group of figures, rather than the more common Latin word "catharsis." The Greek word relates to that collective experience of purgation by pity and fear that Aristotle describes in the *Poetics*. The artist has said of the Greek *katarsis*:

> The Greek word *katarsis* embodies a group of sounds in which I hear metal, the rasp of cutting, the drama of destructions.

It is obvious that the artist's own experience of deliverance after the tragedy of war gave the word's meaning of emotional release a special weight.

The artist has written that in KATARSIS, she wished to leave a sense of anxiety with the viewer:

> KATARSIS is of a material more lasting than life. Perhaps because I hoped that the signs left behind would be for others a lasting anxiety.[7]

Abakanowicz's most powerful and valid outdoor sculptures are those created for contemplation in specific spaces: KATARSIS, NEGEV, SPACE OF STONE, 2002 (p. 62), and AGORA. She has called these works "sacred spaces" and "spaces to experience."

For the spatial arrangement of the thirty-three bronze figures in the space of KATARSIS, Abakanowicz and her husband built a model of the landscape site and moved the figures around. The final arrangement was, for Abakanowicz, a contrast to the "beautified" nature that surrounded them in the sculpture park. KATARSIS's figures suggest both bizarre tree trunks, which emerge from the earth, as well as artistic objects, and as such they stand for a fusion of art and nature. Sensitive to the figure's relation to nature, the artist deliberately left the bronze patina unfinished so that wind, sun, and rain would alter the surface.

In SPACE OF STONE, Abakanowicz's twenty-two-part stone composition created for Grounds For Sculpture, a sculpture garden in New Jersey, the artist's intention was to establish an environment that "we must enter, penetrate, become part of." This work was created out of granite pieces—gray Barre granite and black Philadelphia granite—which had been broken in the quarry in a natural, accidental way, and shows the mysterious, strong texture of the stone. As the artist has said, this texture is similar to that of a "tree trunk, human muscle, or skin. This is nature's confession to her creative powers. Stone never breaks the same way. The shape of the twenty-two elements is the natural result of breaking; when it breaks it shows us its unexpected inside, its hidden mystery of the stone's confession to man. The inside of these stones carries the same story that one finds in man's skin, the bark of a tree, a dry leaf." The artist selected the granite elements because of their textures and then further developed the identity of each piece by flaming the surfaces with a torch.

SPACE OF STONE belongs to a series of Abakanowicz's works permanently installed outdoors: KATARSIS, SPACE OF DRAGON (ten metamorphic bronze animal heads in Korea), UNKNOWN GROWTH (twenty-three shapes of concrete in Lithuania), and UNRECOGNIZED (112 cast-iron figures in Poland). In these outdoor compositions, sculpture is no longer an object to look at but a space to experience and contemplate. Abakanowicz confronts the imagination of man with the imagination of nature. She sees sculpture as a metaphor to express what happens in this interaction which words cannot express.

SPACE OF STONE is outstanding in its symbolism and visual poetry. As in NEGEV, where Abakanowicz invested the roughly geometric disks with an implied movement, so here, in cutting eleven blocks into twenty-two triangles, she has created ways of tilting the jagged pieces. The way the stones meet the earth suggests kinetic energy and action. With its multiple perspectives created by the shifted angles of each stone, the work pulls us into its space so that we can become part of it and learn about our scale and the scale of our surroundings. Abakanowicz spent several years with this broken granite, learning about its nature, the relationship between the twenty-two forms, and the tensions created in space. She has written that each of her works was born of "the chosen space and the chosen material—ideas that would never be born in the artist's studio."

The artist's creation of remarkably expressive edges and surfaces comes from a sense of materials and also from a painful knowledge of mankind in history. The artist speaks of material the way some would speak of a new religion:

> It is fascinating to work with matter, whether wood, or bronze, cement, stone, or iron. One must understand its language, its possibility to express itself and myself. One must unite with it, feel its strength and weakness, penetrate to its essence. The way the stones meet the earth suggests its soul.[8]

Like Boccioni or Maya Lin, Abakanowicz gives great importance to the space between the grouped sculpture's boundaries, or edge and that of life itself—the surrounding environmental space.

Abakanowicz's astonishing work, while it imbues art with a tragic vision, is also, in today's fragmented cosmos, an existential reminder of unity. The artist's thoughtful placing of her works in outdoor settings reminds us that this is the most ennobling way we can "use" art and also nature.

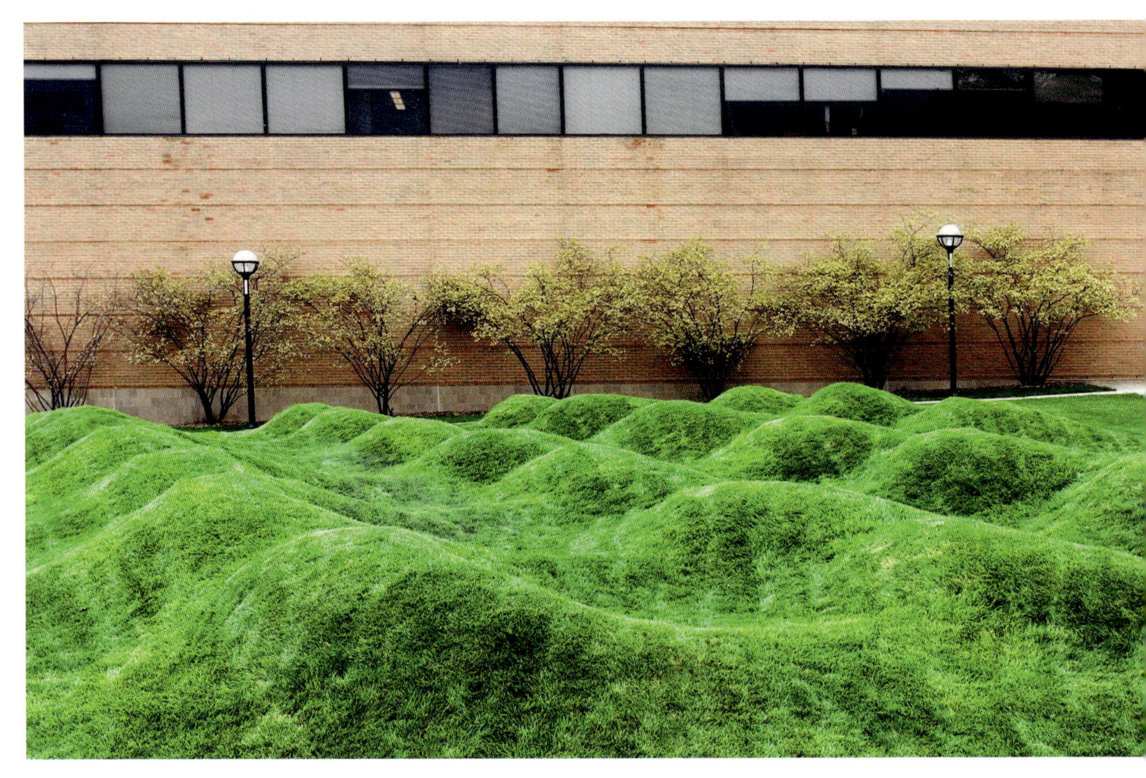

THE CONTEMPORARY EDGE "IN FLUX": WAVEFIELD
*Maya Lin's edges in WAVEFIELD, inspired by the mobile dynamics of the waves of the ocean, are in constant flux.*
*Lin's work, while finite, expresses infinite expansion, without beginning or end.*

Maya Lin, WAVEFIELD, 1995

*Chapter VII*

# MAYA LIN: THE EDGE AS POETIC IDEA

If classical art "contains," Maya Lin's art has contours in constant flux. The form of Maya Lin's VIETNAM VETERANS MEMORIAL (1982) is not that of a sculpture but that of an edge. She has written: "I never looked at the memorial as a wall, an object, but as an edge to the earth . . . cutting the earth, opening the earth and creating a dialogue directly with the landscape."[1] When designing the VIETNAM VETERANS MEMORIAL, Lin realized that her artistic vision was more "on an emotional level than a formal one." She began thinking about her design for the memorial as a student at Yale School of Architecture, as she watched stonecutters carving by hand the names of Yale students killed in the Vietnam War. Lin found herself moved by the edges of the carved individual names:

> I had never been able to resist touching the names cut into those marble walls, and no matter how busy or crowded the place is . . . a sense of quiet, a reverence always surrounds those names.[2]

The force of the VIETNAM VETERANS MEMORIAL comes from the artist's gesture of cutting a gigantic rift in the earth. Lin has described the huge black granite slabs, each 200 feet long, as a gash of pain that must heal in time. Although an abstract work, Lin describes it as the first step in a ten-year period of work that dealt with a "dialogue with landscape."

In all of Lin's work, whether for galleries or outdoor spaces, she has been inspired by a passion for the landscape. She has said in her autobiographical book *Boundaries* that her grasp of the plastic and the pure in nature came from her father, a potter, and also from the influence of the two- to three-thousand-year-old Hopewell and Adena Indian burial mounds in Ohio, where she was born.

> They have probably helped form a foundation of who I am and my work as much as have the hills of southeastern Ohio, which were incredibly soft and undulating.[3]

Lin has described her aesthetic as a mixture of Shaker and Japanese.

Her aesthetics goals also include what she has called a "desire to walk people through a space; with a modulation of height, materiality, texture, and light, you can make people feel happier, and calmer."

In the VIETNAM VETERANS MEMORIAL, Lin wanted viewers to experience pain and loss, and then be able to be healed. She stuck to her guns when many well-known architects protested her choice of polished black granite, and only a thin edge, calling them "too feminine." They wanted her to make the work massive, heavy, whereas the artist always saw the wall as pure surface. "As I saw it, I cut into the earth and polished its open edge."[4] Lin sees the design as experimental and cathartic.

Lin's work, whether public or for galleries, reveals her perception of the edge as neither containing nor expanding but in constant flux. She views her work as a continuous dialogue with nature's poetic, elusive edges. She sees water as a perfect metaphor for the idea of boundary/edge and the absence of edge; waves in the ocean are always in the process of destroying an old edge and creating a new one, as they change shape due to the movement of the tides.

Lin has created monuments out of this elusive and protean material, water; indeed, her feeling for water's qualities animates many of her works. "I stared at the ocean for hours, trying to find a beginning and an end. But of course there is none." Her poetic grasp of water's tactile and symbolic qualities are central to the CIVIL RIGHTS MEMORIAL, 1989 (p. 98) in Montgomery, Alabama, as well as the SHIFT IN THE STREAM (1995–1997). These are transformed when the viewer touches the water.

Lin's latest project, STORM KING WAVEFIELD (2008–2009) is a permanent, site-specific work covering 11 acres at the Storm King Art Center in Mountainville, New York. Seven undulating hills of earth, 300–370 feet long and 10–18 feet high, are the largest of her site-specific landscapes. "It's part of a study that started with looking at a simple water wave," Lin said. The monumental STORM KING WAVEFIELD is the latest and third of the "Wavefields." Lin created a naturally made drainage system and trees and grasses were planted that stress the long lasting or sustainability of the project. Lin planted grasses ranging from Creeping Red Fescus to Canada Bluegrass, clover, white daisies, and yellow-flowered partridge pea; Lin plans to plant 260 indigenous trees.[5] Simultaneous to the opening of WAVEFIELD, Storm King is presenting an exhibition, *Maya Lin: Bodies of Water*, featuring a dozen works that show the artist's use of water as a material in her work.

Eight years ago, when the artist first visited Storm King, she found herself drawn to an area which was formerly a gravel pit. The artist has said she wanted to culminate the series with a field that literally, when you were in it, you became lost. "I see the work as an immersive environment that blurs the distinction between viewer and artwork, and artwork and nature."[6]

One of her favorite site-specific works is the CIVIL RIGHTS MEMORIAL.

Lin's approach to her art is daring and idiosyncratic. On the plane to Montgomery, Lin read the words of Dr. Martin Luther King, Jr.: "We are not satisfied and we will not be satisfied until justice rolls down like waters and righteousness like a mighty stream." Right away, Lin decided that the memorial would be about water.[7] Water is par excellence the material with mysterious edges and Lin designed the CIVIL RIGHTS MEMORIAL to orchestrate King's words with images and the realities of water: powerful, continuous, yet not fully visible. Just when we think we see a defining contour, we in fact see many contours, which are dissolving constantly, in flux.

Words and events are often as influential as landscape and aesthetics. Lin's design for the CIVIL RIGHTS MEMORIAL started out as two elements in black granite, a table and a curved wall, 9 feet high and 40 feet long. The memorial has an upper and a lower plaza. The water source for the wall is a reflecting pool in the upper plaza: the table emits its own water film, a thin, continually moving layer of water, which bubbles gently out of its off-center hub. The monument gains its power from the veil of water which flows continuously over the front edge of the pool down the huge wall. Inscribed on this huge black wall are the Bible-based words of Dr. King with their arresting water imagery.

The water in this monument is as carefully controlled as Lin's choice of a particular black granite, and her decision to use a specific stone engraver to inscribe the words. The movement of the water across the top of the table is so slow as to be almost imperceptible. In this way Lin made the water seem almost static until visitors touched the watery surface, or until the water reaches the edge and turns, appearing to flow upside down until it reaches the base. This particular black granite, when dry, is totally matte, while when touched with water, it becomes reflective. In Lin's words, the water "transforms the work."

When the work was dedicated, people gathered for a ceremony which included victims and families of victims, and literally, human tears "fell upon the water." Lin intended that this would connect the water imagery in the Bible—which had so inspired King—with the actual liquid of human tears. Lin also had a brief history of the era inscribed on the table; for a visual artist, this unusual emphasis on words and facts in history defines the historical aspect of her work. In the artist's own words, "it describes what was in effect a people's movement, not just the work of a few well-known individuals, showing how individual people helped to change history." In order to emphasize a theme about racial equality and inequality, Lin used the idea of asymmetrical balances. The curved stairway on the right side of the plaza is visually balanced by the circular water table located on the left side. Lin chose to make the table asymmetrical at its base in order to break the symmetry of the existing Montgomery architecture.

In Lin's internal surfaces and external contours, she uses asymmetry as a way to give art its magic and power. Lin has written: "You push the forms slightly off kilter, because what we think we see is symmetry, yet nothing in nature is technically symmetrical." This echoes Noguchi's statement that symmetrical, geometric forms remove themselves from nature too abruptly.

Lin is best known for monumental public sculptures but she also makes outstanding sculptural installations and gallery-scaled works conceived for an exhibition rather than a specific site. She fuses the tools of technology with her own poetic sensibility. This was obvious in her 1998 show *Topologies*, organized by the Southeastern Center for Contemporary Art (SECCA), by curator Jeff Fleming.

Installed at NYU's Grey Gallery, the sculptures presented Lin's view of landscape—in the category of art yet closely connected to life. For example, in ROCK FIELD (1997), spotlights on the ceiling dramatized the forty-two stones which had been spaced on a riverbed. Lin placed vessels at irregular spatial intervals on a birch plywood floor that was installed specially for the exhibition. These beautiful objects have multiple associations: from gigantic drops of rain to oversized pebbles on a beach.

One of Lin's masterpieces was commissioned in 1993 for the Aerospace Building, University of Michigan in Ann Arbor. This work reflects what Lin calls a pure love of landscape: "It's trying to bring indoors the feeling you get when you might look over a rippling sand dune or the ocean waves." WAVEFIELD (p. 68) was indeed inspired as much by the ocean as by the artist's study of fluid dynamics. Students can sit, while reading and studying, inside the sculpture with their backs against mounds of grass that reach up to 4 to 6 feet. Lin has said that WAVEFIELD, which extends over 10,000 square feet, has the sense of being contained as an object until the viewer enters the field, and then the scale, in the artist's words, "takes over as a field, rather than an object."

Out of WAVEFIELD grew Lin's floor piece entitled TOPOGRAPHIC LANDSCAPE (1997), for her traveling exhibition *Topographies*. For TOPOGRAPHIC LANDSCAPE, Lin created an undulating field from long curved strips of particleboard, each cut by Lin and her assistant to produce a "wave edge." This work shows that when Lin arranged them side by side in a room, they form a large area of soft mounds and curves which fall and rise.

Lin compels us to look at landscape in a totally new way. In her vision, rocks are made of glass, and rolling hills might resemble ocean waves, or, when in a gallery, plywood curves. Seeing art, or landscape, from different angles creates new perspectives in the viewer. Whether in galleries or large architectural installations, this perspective of constant flux is both a goal and achievement of Lin's.

In SHIFT IN THE STREAM (Des Moines, Iowa) one first experiences the work as a barely perceptible trickling of water down the two-story high glass walls of the lobby. As in the CIVIL RIGHTS

MEMORIAL, the water is carefully controlled so that several streams of water flow down these glass walls. Changes in water flow and location give the appearance of the haphazard. The wall was made by breaking smaller sections of plaster into a zigzagging pattern, and then connecting the broken edges to form a continuous rift. The structure is, literally, a fissure or crack, but it is also like a winding river seen from above.

Lin's brilliance as an artist lies in her bold and unconventional approach, a mix of philosophy, aesthetic style, and commitment to the earth, made manifest in her technical inventions.

Lin's words are obviously the most apt to express her vision:

> Maybe art can focus, point out something in the natural world that you might not notice. For me, that's what this is fundamentally about. I have a deeper love and respect for the land and I've been inspired by that, although I'm not trying to mimic it completely. I walk off. I get inspiration and do something that I feel is personally very right.

Lin, like Noguchi, uses art to make the landscape part of us.

*Chapter VIII*

# ROBERT LOBE: THE BAROQUE ABSTRACT

Robert Lobe's sculptures astonish, in this déjà-vu art world, with their grandeur and originality of vision. Of his wall pieces and freestanding tree sculptures, Lobe says that he returned to nature in a new way, more conscious of the sublime—a sublime both fearful and beautiful. This attitude towards nature places him as a Northern Romantic; in his treatment of landscape, which magically fuses the scientific and the ecstatic, there are analogies to American Transcendentalism.

Lobe, who has aptly said "edge is the key to mass and volume," showed many years ago a hyperawareness of edge as an expressive force. From no two vantage points does any part of his work appear the same. Lobe's writings about the sculptural edge, mass, and their relation to nature grow out of and express the work:

> My inspiration for the edge was not only Bernini but also David Smith. I was impressed by the way the planes abut, leaving a gap, filled by a weld, catching a shadow, becoming an edge. As I wrap sheets of metal around nature's irregular shapes, often the edge falls across a plane. The holes in my work are also edge—another way to identify presence . . . Art has to do with the invention of our desires. Something that says, now we're getting a bit closer . . . To use the forms of nature requires respect of the art and science that govern its laws of growth and change.[1]

Lobe's exhibit in California in 2004 showed important developments from his previous work. A contrapuntal relation between realistic nature and abstraction has always been fundamental to his sculptures. But his new works, both the bas-reliefs and the freestanding tree forms, are far more abstract—further from the motif—than any of Lobe's other works from the past thirty years. In both genres, the artist now "rearranges" the nature that he selects to be shaped and hammered into art.[2]

VINE, 1999 (p. 103) demonstrates this move towards greater abstraction. It is composed in a freer way, with a virtuoso treatment of surface. Lobe says that his use of much thicker aluminum sheets, which he anodizes, allows him to work the aluminum "like clay." Thus he can create voluptuously articulated surfaces, with whorls of molten metal and labyrinths of lines within a terrain. Truly "abstracted" from the original object or site in nature, this work is more Lobe's conception of particular natural elements than literal recreations of those elements themselves.

The new wall pieces with the extravagant silhouette and surface that is both meticulous and sensuous is emphatically Baroque in its theatricality, plunging diagonals, and complex patterns of movement. The edges, Baroque in character, alternate between sharpness and fluidity, giving the work a dramatic tactility. As in VINE, Lobe adapts the technique of radically opposing directional movement: one mass of volume moves left, the other right, creating a mood of energy and majesty.

Lobe's work resembles Noguchi's in its intense drama and tactility, and in contrasting raw nature to the intercessions of art. The silhouettes of Lobe's works often recall the bizarre shapes and edges of Chinese scholars' rocks, as well as the plunging diagonals in Bernini's treatment of drapery. The way Lobe uses aluminum, an extremely responsive material, steeps his work in mystery. Light is an active poetic protagonist, augmenting theatricality as it moves over a terrain of edges at times fierce, at times serene.

The viewer begins with a sense of Lobe's homage to the natural world. Then, close-up, one sees an infinity of mark-making: hammered, chiseled, and pointed details, which add up to a volcanic textured surface, a microcosm of pitted and fissured matter. The work is contradictory: while it has a taut centeredness, it is also spatially voluminous, with an insistence on penetrating the viewer's space. HARMONY RIDGE, 1996 (p. 104) has a dark and menacing plasticity and is orchestrated on an immense scale. If cloudlike and beatific, this work also evokes nature's *terribilità*.

The wall sculptures embody the themes of growth and change so common in Baroque sculpture. Of the bas-reliefs, CIRCLE (2005) continues the triumphantly Baroque tone, compelling in vertiginous stance and lush, complex rhythms, while others take a decidedly classical stance, serene and balanced. Lobe sees the bas-reliefs such as

PAGE I, VOL. 11, 1999 (p. 79) with its elegantly broken, irregular edges as "pages from a notebook—the notebook of nature." The analogy to pages or drawings is apt, as Lobe, with his hammering tools, "draws" on the aluminum sheets.[3]

As concentrated distillations of a whole, these works have immense power. Lobe knows that the fragment has an undiluted energy and plastic unity that the whole may not. In these works, the formal qualities themselves—the volumes, the mass, the lines, the edges, the rhythms—are so precise as to symbolize the whole. Surely these surfaces, where light makes the forms dissolve and merge, create an image of a world in movement. The surfaces reveal a substructure of substance and material. Stark and calligraphic, Lobe's rhythmic groupings of trees, as in HARMONY RIDGE (1996, Reston, Virginia), shows an inward and perceptual relationship to nature. To the artist, these works are "interior landscapes."

There is a spare and linear elegance to the tree works and a spatial symmetry that suggests an Eastern aesthetic. In the wall pieces, Lobe gives the energies of art and nature equal power; in the tree works, he suggests that art has the greater voice, and the accents—stones on the branches—are like music, creating a spare rhythm.

Lobe's CIRCLE demonstrates what he called an American tendency to hold the "resolution in balance" in his creation of a molten, menacing surface, which appears, like a tidal wave, at its highest point, about to break. This sense of a reenactment of nature's energies, as well as the turbulence of the surface, recalls those of Rodin. Lobe recently said: "I want to convey the discovery, the unexpectedness of the familiar." In CIRCLE Lobe's mark making seems freer, more massive. CIRCLE's monumental forms are more volatile in contour and edge. The work has a Dionysian choreography of plunging heavy bronze curves, recalling, in force and repetition, waves of an angry sea.

As Barry Schwabsky pointed out some years ago in *Art in America*, most sculptors who supposedly deal with nature have no spiritual or philosophical relationship to it. The United States may possess vast expanses of extraordinary natural landscape, but we Americans do not believe in it. While we are at home in nature, nature is not our home.[4]

Lobe's affirmation over twenty-five years ago of the ancient but forgotten truth of man's interdependence with nature relates to American Transcendentalism. He has certainly achieved his own transcendental sublime. His unique achievement recalls the words of Leonardo da Vinci, who praised artists "capable of disputing and contending with nature." Lobe's sculpture suggests a possible mediation between human existence and the larger natural world. While poetic, his work is about the destructiveness of nature and the destructiveness of man. He is an important sculptor not only for his formal qualities but for the authenticity and relevance of his vision.[5]

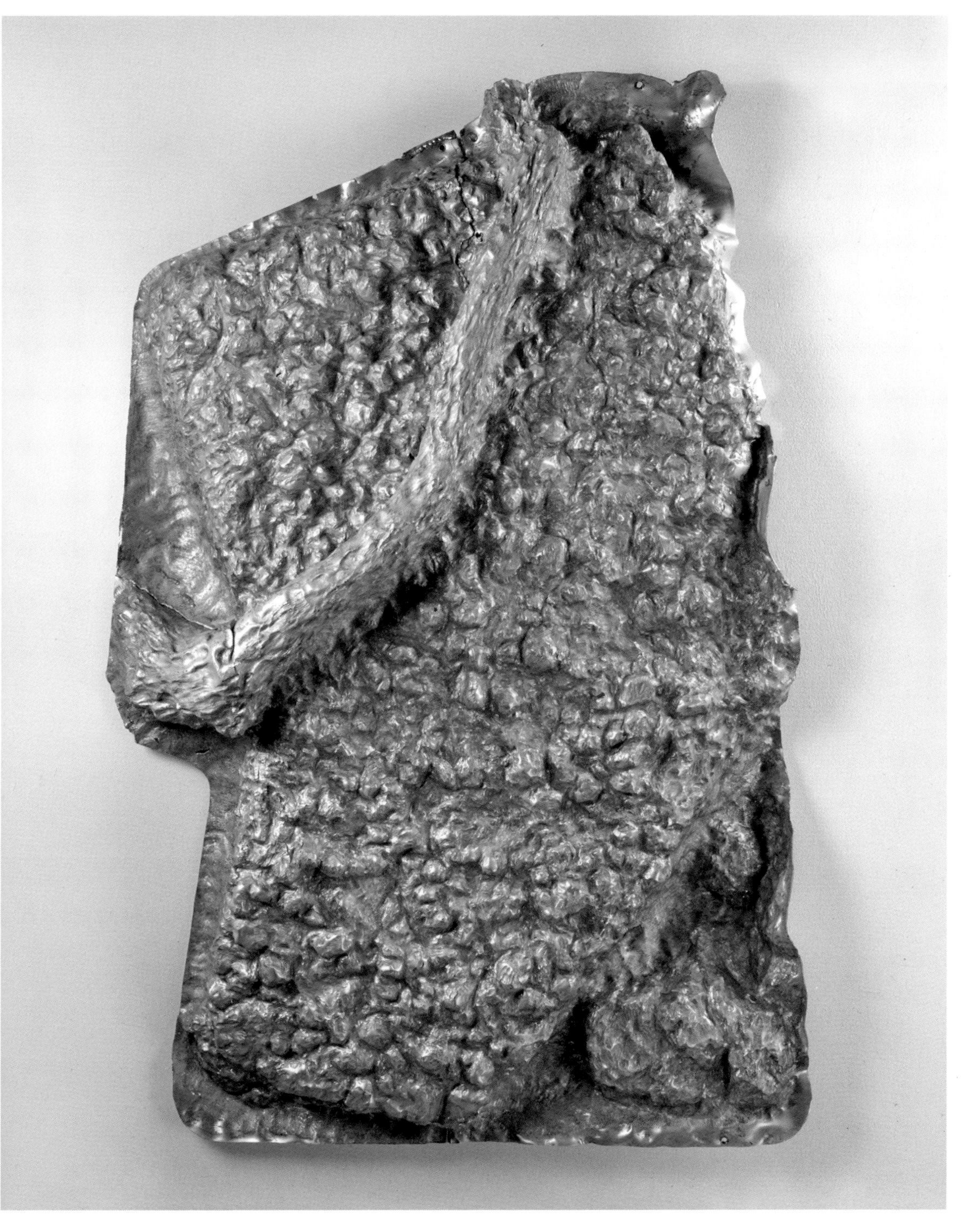

Robert Lobe, PAGE I,VOL. 11, 1999

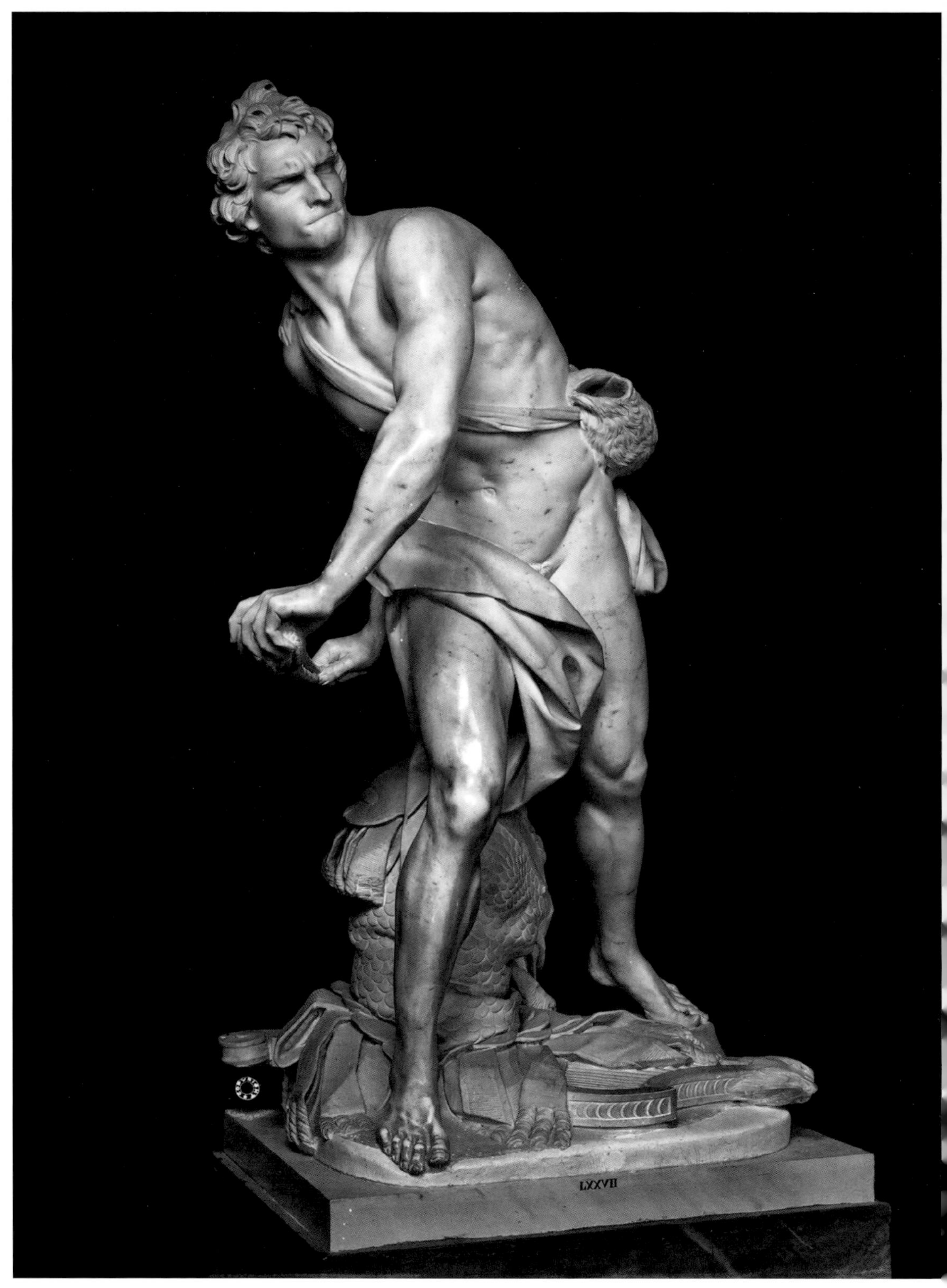


Gianlorenzo Bernini, DAVID, 1623–1624

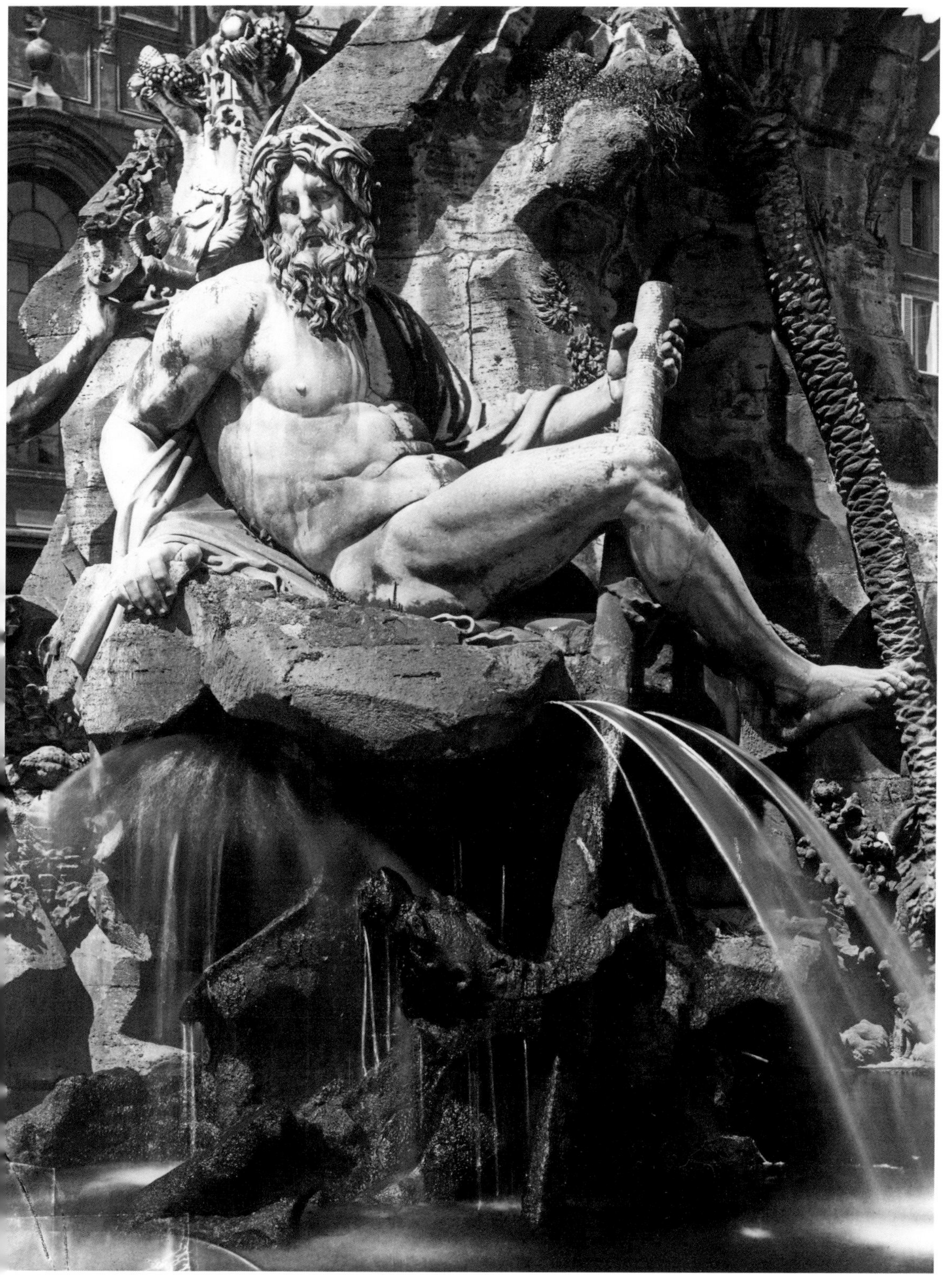

Gianlorenzo Bernini, FOUNTAIN OF THE FOUR RIVERS, detail, 1651

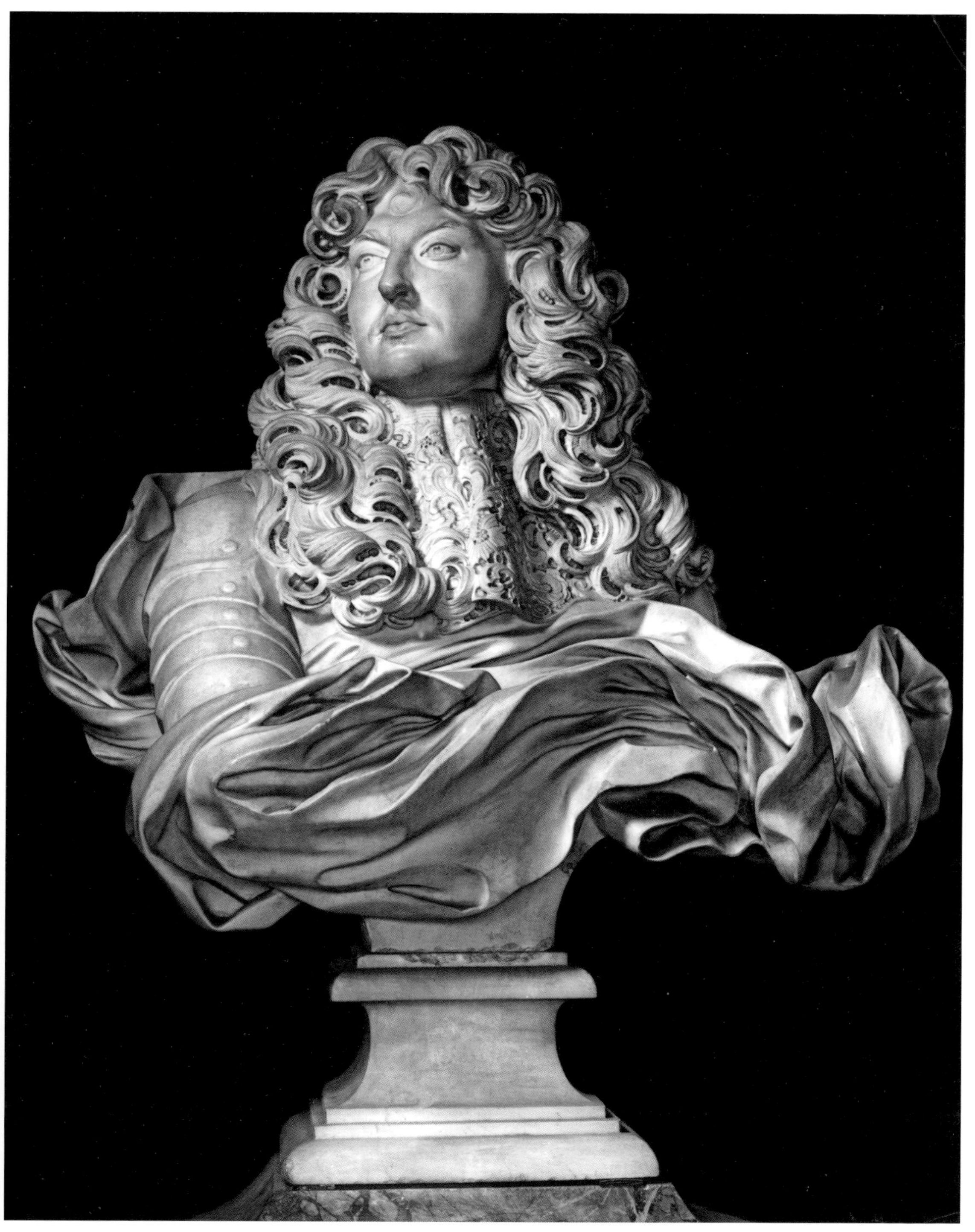

Gianlorenzo Bernini, LOUIS XIV, 1665

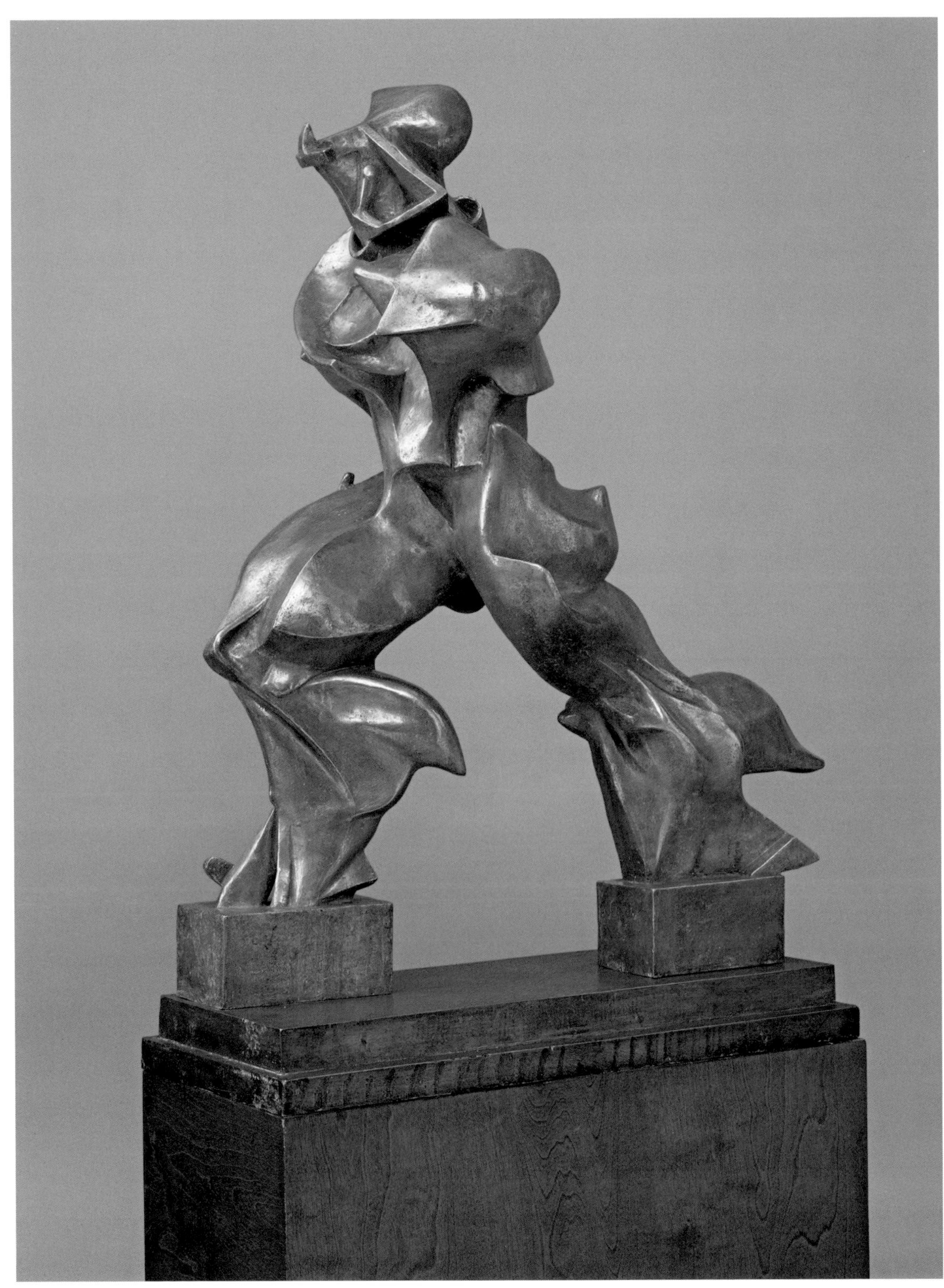

Umberto Boccioni, UNIQUE FORMS OF CONTINUITY IN SPACE, 1913

Isamu Noguchi, VERTICAL VIEW, late 1960s

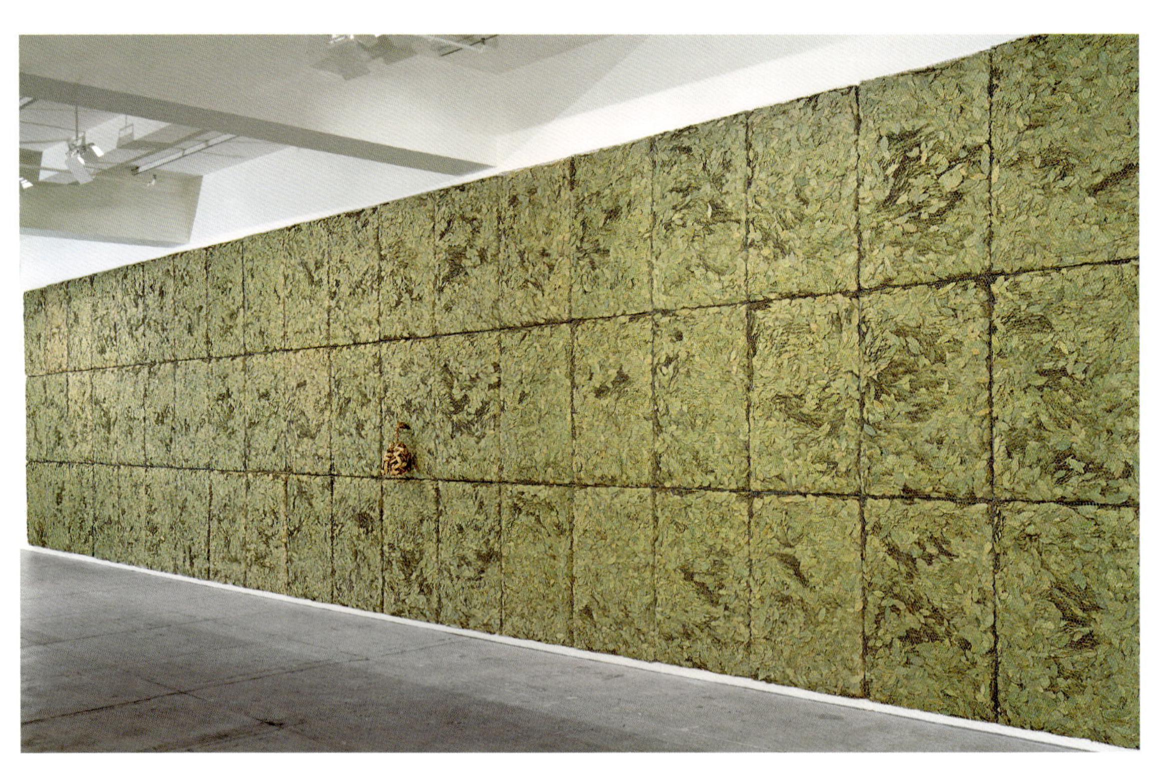

Giuseppe Penone, RESPIRARE OMBRA, 2003

*Chapter IX*

# GIUSEPPE PENONE: THE BREATH, THE TOUCH, THE TREE

Penone's art "begins" in a place we can see, physically and conceptually, but frequently we are not able to tell where it ends. Why? Because Penone's edges, like those of Lin, Boccioni, and Zhang, are in constant flux. They ask the question: How can breath, water, and time assume substance? Their contours sometimes are barely visible, occurring in phenomena such as the human breath (*soffio*), barely tactile fingerprints, the continual growth of a tree (*l'albero*), water, and time. A famous series of works entitled RESPIRARE OMBRA (p. 86), involving the massing of laurel leaves in mesh cages, and extending over 52 feet in length, in fact goes back to a series of some twenty-five years ago on the theme of breath.

In October 2008, Penone showed new monumental works that affirmed with striking originality the theme of man's apprehension of nature. In these works, the edges, whether in bronze, leather, stone, or *grafite*, are distinctly more dimensional, tactile, visible, but retain that tenuous mystery Penone sees in nature. In RIFLESSO DEL BRONZO (2005) the eight-paneled bronze serial work, overall 52 feet in length (each panel 5 feet x 31/2 feet), Penone dramatizes nature's tiniest details (and processes) in massive proportions. This work extends from the first bronze handmade plate, a bronze mirror whose surface is the result of Penone's hands and intensive contact with the surface of the work: it then proceeds to a succession of bronze casts (each new cast maintaining the imperfections inherent in the previous one).

The contours/edges of each bronze panel are dramatically irregular, and 2 inches wide, like sheets of ancient paper forming a tablet.

SCRIGNO, 2007 (p. 61) a large 20 foot x 9 foot leather work evokes both a huge, stretched animal skin and a view of an erupting labyrinthine surface of the planet Earth seen from another world. It affirms once again Penone's perspective of microcosm/macrocosm. Edges which are in reality tiny become vast, contours which are vast and immeasurable become finite.

In a seemingly contradictory mode, Penone's show at the Drawing Center in 2004 affirmed edge-as-surface, and, on both a micro and macrocosmic way, ten examples of "touch," in one drawing for each of his fingerprints. In the words of the artist:

> The basic idea is touch . . . the image becomes a sensitive surface that corresponds to the contact I had . . . As if there were a giant hand that occupies the space and leaves fingerprints on the ten sheets of paper . . . an extension of my skin in the space.

As critic Briony Fer writes:

> If touch and the haptic have historically been the concerns of sculpture, then in a sense Penone makes every surface, however seemingly insignificant, dramatize the tactile space between volumes and things.[1]

In the fact that Penone's edges can only be intuited subtly, only briefly touched as "finite," he recalls Maya Lin, whose sculptures are often inspired by those edges in nature that only "define" themselves briefly, like the continuously changing edges of waves in the sea. We cannot "see" a tree growing; we can only "see" ways of measuring a tree's growth after the growth has already taken place—a subject that often occupies Penone. The edges that attract Lin and Penone are those of the infinite and boundless. Penone has demonstrated a belief that patterns of human consciousness resemble the rhythms of the surrounding landscape.

Penone's works based on the metaphor of human breath began in 1978. In BREATH 5, now in the Tate Gallery, London, a large work over 5 feet high made of terracotta, the artist was concerned with the sculptural realization of the natural process of breathing. The bulging brown form represents the imagined shape of the artist's own breath as he blows down towards the ground. The shape recalls a giant amphora. The zigzagging contours of the billowing sculpture's edges symbolize the breath moving around the artist's body, and the long vertical gash down the side of the jar-like form was made by the artist pushing his blue-jean clad leg into the side of the sculpture. The structure at the jar's top is a literal mold made from the artist's own teeth in the clay. Commenting on the sources of this 1978 "Breath" series, Penone wrote:

According to a myth the creator of man was the God Khnum who is represented as a potter shaping man on his wheel. In another myth Athena breathes life into men whom Prometheus had made from clay and water.

With Penone's inclusion both of his mouth and his leg in ultra-realistic form, and breath, by contrast, in a symbolic way, he made a poetic work of art that stands for both the act of creation and the man that has been created. Penone's *soffio* sculptures were also inspired by Leonardo da Vinci's drawings of how he imagined air currents of a single human breath. Leonardo had based his designs on patterns of running water.

Penone had ingeniously adapted Leonardo's idea and association of breath with the act of creation and, in addition, made his burgeoning terracotta form with a vaginal cavity evoke a female fertility symbol, thus fusing varied images of life forms as they grow.

For another twenty-five years Penone continued to dramatize thoughts and sensuous inventions on the theme of breath in works that depend on subtle meanings of sculptural edges. The artist has observed that in cool weather, our breath produces white, thick air, so viscous and dense that it casts a shadow, and has solidity and mass. That air is a solid body as well as a gas may be a surprising thought, as breath seems so ephemeral . . . But it is not altogether ephemeral, for it is true—as the Spanish poet Jabes has written, that "one makes shadows when breathing." Penone's sculptures of two related series entitled RESPIRARE OMBRA and SOFFIO DI FOGLIE dramatize man's breath and nature's breath—symbolized as wind and as movement—as being interdependent, and as infinite and "edgeless" phenomena in nature.

As man breathes, he becomes aware of participating in the breathing, changing rhythms of the universe. For example, in his magnificent 2001–2002 installations, RESPIRARE OMBRA, shown in Avignon and New York, he returned to the breath idea originated in 1878 with panache and poetry. Extravagantly spatial, the work covered one entire wall of New York's Marian Goodman Gallery from floor to ceiling. It consisted of 488 wire mesh boxes, filled with laurel leaves. Because the leaves are loosely amassed within each mesh cage, they shift around and, with each shift, necessarily change their many "edges" and planes, creating 52 feet of chiaroscuro as new dark hollows appear where a mass of leaves had been. This remarkable work illustrates Penone's genius for creating a monumental homage to the transient.

As opposed to many artists, where photographs of the works may be more compelling than the works themselves, Penone produces sensuously valid, large scale, and permanent art works ironically based on nature's transient realities. Penone's works are based on universal, humanistic truths, classical myths; his sculptures do not, therefore, dissociate themselves from culture (as minimalism often had) but succeed in embodying in art and culture the dialectic of the natural and the human.

In 1999 Penone returned to working with another "invisible" edge—that of water—as he had done memorably in 1981, in ETRE FLEUVE. In LINEE D'ACQUA (2004, bronze and water), he again did a large scale gallery work which not only conjures nature but dramatically brings a large body of water into an art gallery, in a large rectangular pool. This poetic work hauntingly acts as a microcosm of a larger landscape. The 14 foot branch delivers a continuous but slow sequence of drops of water into the pool. The isolated drops evoke a lonely and romantic feeling, while a beautifully colored abstract pattern forms on the bottom of the pool from the interaction of the water and the metal. Simultaneously, rippling patterns from the drops create a constant movement, which changes the surface edges of the water.

LINEE D'ACQUA also affirmed Penone's central metaphor of the tree as growth, for inside the large bronze tree is another tree, an image of the embryo trees Penone carved from actual trees in his native Liguria.

Trees, because of their skin-like bark through which air breathes and which is also impermeable to water, have always been central to mythology and worshipped by many cultures. Penone's later works with trees were prefigured by his well-known early work entitled TREE OF 12 METERS (1980–1982), which was made by scraping away the outer layers of wood from a complete felled tree to reveal the form of the tree at an earlier stage of its growth.

The artist himself has written extensively about wood, and about trees. One of his favorite stories tells of a Japanese Emperor who is presented with a very valuable string instrument made of cedar. No one could play the instrument, until a man picked up the cedar instrument, and by plucking the strings, was able to tell the story of the cedar tree from which the musical instrument derived. Then the music produced was of great beauty.

Penone feels an affinity to this story when he gouges his trees, measuring time as he counts the annual rings as they change.

Penone's signature theme, over the years, has been man's interdependence and inseparability from the landscape. Penone is interested in the "small changes that occur to the surface of things"—not unlike Rodin's remark about the millions of changes that occur between the "belly and the thigh." Penone's tactile diagrams vastly expand the idea of sculpture to chart even the slightest sensory experience as if it were an intricate "map" of the pressure points between skin and surface.

The edges created by Penone's tactile diagrams are infinitesimal, and the viewer can barely feel them with his or her own fingers, but they form tiny edges or ridges.

Penone's work entitled PROPAGAZIONE affirmed an analogy between a fingerprint's lines and those lines which oscillated through a tree trunk (shown both at Konrad Fischer in Dusseldorf and in 1999 at Santiago de Compostela). Because of his concept of the imprint, Penone frequently changes "tangential and oblique" moves within works and between works, or what the artist sometimes has called "transfers." With his concept of interdependence, the artist frequently changes the roles of subject and object, between himself and his sculpture, the landscape and the art. As though he were something other than the artist himself, Penone often withdraws from his role as a sculptor.

To put Penone in a category of landscape art is misleading about his originality of vision and unusual achievement. His work, unlike much conceptual art, is monumental in its visual essence, as well as in the idea. Like one of his first sculptures, his hand grasping a tree trunk, his work is concerned with taking in the universe, as grasped by his own body and mind, of his own personal existence, and of the most basic gestures, traces, or imprints of his human existence, from his eyelids, fingerprints, and the span of his own hand. His subject could be called the human being as part of the natural universe.

His series EYELIDS are an example of his extending his own body, his eyelid's imprint onto gelatin, and then projecting it, hugely magnified, onto a surface after which he traces the "pressure points." As the artist has said, "the eyelid separates touch from vision." He ends up making a slight edge or texture out of what he sees projected.

In Penone's view, man is both culture and nature in one. His view of the artwork, of sculpture, and of a sculpture's edge is similar to his view of nature as something forever unfolding and becoming, not what he calls a "cultural product" but an ongoing part of nature.

In his work called ANATOME, from the mid-1990s, made of Carrara marble, Penone has tried to determine what forms the internal structure of the marble. What the artist tries to do is make the veins in the white Carrara marble come to life, to give the inner structure of the anatomy within the stone a corporeal existence once again. He accomplishes this by hollowing out the veins in the marble in some areas, and in other areas by freeing them.

Penone is that oddity among artists: rather than inventing art that departs from reality, he sees himself as making his art "along the surface of reality," making even the most inconsequential details visible. This artist is interested in the reality of mankind associated with the world—a world quintessentially known through a sense of touch. After Rodin, but in a conceptual mode, Penone is the sculptor most passionately involved in touch.

*Chapter X*

# JIAN JUN ZHANG

Jian Jun Zhang, born in Shanghai in 1955, has been told recently that his work is "too Western" and also that his work is "too Eastern." Indeed, the artist sees his life and work as a "river of cultures."[1] He now lives and exhibits both in the United States and in China. A teacher at New York University, Zhang also brings his students to study at the University of Shanghai. These students learn how to use Chinese ink as well as to continue to study Western painting, sculpture, and video.

His works examine historical and cultural ideas in a frame of reference that is modern and Western, but also affirms basic truths of Chinese philosophy: the balance of stillness (*jing*) and movement (*dong*), the Five Elements, and continuity through change. His artistic vision is both realistic and symbolic, and his mind seems to turn again and again to three elements that are metaphors for the link between China and the West—water, scholars' rocks, and ink.

Zhang's artistic method is a trenchant example of surrealist displacement; the artist forces his Chinese historical images to make a huge aesthetic leap from their original contemplative function as scholars' rocks in ninth-century Chinese gardens into the modern replicas of silicone rubber. The modern scholars' rocks, sometimes pink, sometimes blue, are cast from the original black mountainous rock that the artist purchased in China, but then transformed in material and context, in a commercial American gallery.

Of his use of materials, both the ancient rock and the new silicone rubber, Zhang has said: "I feel I am borrowing the energy of those materials, colors, and textures."[2] In creating his scholars' rocks or modern gardens, Zhang fuses "two energies."

Zhang said, of the original ninth-century rock that he bought:

> To buy a rock like that is like being attracted to a particular person—a total personality, with a mood, a distinct aura. The rock I chose, rather than being a solid mass, has beautiful perforations and myriad richness of curved openings. The skin texture is smooth, but rough—alive with formal incident.[3]

The many sculptures that Zhang has cast from the original rock that he purchased, displaced from their original function, are surreal, visual markers of time.

The artist, like Maya Lin and Isamu Noguchi, thinks of water—a watery flow—as the core structure of many of his works, whose end is not visible in the beginning. His rocks of ink are fountain-like and impermanent, moving into unpredictable, changing shapes. He says:

> The form of human culture changes in response to the evolving times, ideology, and global politics. The present continually wears away, and is replaced by the new. At the same time, a portion of the old is retained.[4]

Zhang observes that each period of art has its signature edges and lines: ancient Chinese art had curves and whorls, while the Bauhaus was characterized by straight lines. Zhang sees today's irregular curves as relating to the computer and Frank Gehry's architecture.

In his astonishing installation entitled SUMI-INK GARDEN OF RE-CREATION, 2002 (p. 106) created for the 4th Shanghai Biennale, he fused traditional aspects with a postmodern irony. For the traditional aspect, Zhang followed the conventions of the architectural style of Chinese scholar gardens. In the center, Zhang installed six Tai-Hu rocks, reaching up to a height of 10 feet. The "modern" aspect was that these huge rocks were made out of solid sumi-ink. Then he had water pumped from the reservoir at the base of the three smaller rocks. Once at the top, the water trickled down the exterior and returned to the container. In SUMI-INK GARDEN OF RE-CREATION, Zhang used water's invisible edges as a material, along with ink, fish, and antique bricks to form the work. SUMI-INK GARDEN OF RE-CREATION is extant to this day, and continues to change its outer and inner edges as the water, piped into the huge sumi-ink structures, slowly erodes the original ink contours. As time elapses, the rocks continue to gradually wear away. The artist took photographs periodically to record the process of time eroding the ink rocks, showing how the water becomes blacker and blacker, as it becomes permeated over time, with ink. In this masterwork, Zhang makes the viewer confront the past in a sensuous present form. The work has an extreme and eccentric appearance, but in its ordering of volumes and subtle palette of grays, blacks, and beiges, the sculptural installation has a calm balance.

In his large sculptures of solid ink or resin, and ink drawings inspired by water and by architecture, Zhang's art explores how art's edges, continuously changing, can show or mirror changes in society.

In a series of painted photographs entitled TIME CHAPTER: CHELSEA (2004), Zhang experimented with changing a building's contours to show how it changes in time, and how these changes reflect the given society. In these photographs, using oil and graphite, the artist's contours manipulate existing architecture as in his recent alterations of a historic building in China. In the style of the Hui School of Architecture, located in Hong Tzun Village in the Southern Anhui Province, this building was built during the Ming dynasty, around 1500 CE. Zhang describes his alteration of the actual building and the reflecting pool as a societal landscape. He added subtly curved and obliquely angled forms which rise from one side of the building, a change that is not reflected in the water. In Zhang's additions of curvy sculptural stylizations to the blocky roofline of a brick building, he evokes Frank Gehry's swooping concave and convex buildings—lines that characterize twenty-first-century postmodernist forms.

Zhang often takes values and ideas from an idealized past and turns them into metaphors in a precarious postmodern present. For example, in WHERE DO WE COME FROM? WHERE ARE WE GOING? and 2000 YEARS OF MOTION, he invented unearthly, futuristic forms, half humanoid, half column-like, and motorized which wandered around the gallery space. These works embody the artist's idea that the articulation of time is also differentiation of space. They also reflect Zhang's idea that lines of a culture contain and express its meaning, and that our era is marked by irregular curves. The bulbous volumes and swelling profiles slyly evoke the human form: these odd totems paradoxically recall both Bernini's twisting bronze *baldacchino* for St. Peter's Church and Brancusi's ENDLESS COLUMN.

Zhang's humanoid columns create a disjunctive jolt by mixing periods of time and styles. The artist set these objects in motion as each movement marks a different second in time, and, as in a dance performance, every move changes the entire space. They are silent, somnambulant, moving at different velocities and in different directions.

The work is as random and seemingly unplanned as MOUNTAIN AND RIVER is balanced and structured (p. 108).

The use of materials is at the core of Zhang's work where there is a dual reality: stone, water, and ink as natural facts, and stone, water, and ink as symbols. With MOUNTAIN AND RIVER, shown in 2003 in Houston, Zhang dramatized these three symbols, merging a personal vocabulary with the cultural. Of water, the artist has written:

> Since my childhood, living near the river in Shanghai, water and the rhythm of water have influenced my work. I have always kept fish tanks in the city environment. There is an analogy between the way the goldfish change the dynamic of water, and art objects change the structure of space.

Ink, for the artist, like water, has always had a personal symbolism since Zhan's early childhood in China, and has thus figured in many of his works. As a child, he saw his father practice calligraphy every morning before going to work. He has written that ink represents the cultural and spiritual consciousness of humankind.

Zhang installed the breathtakingly beautiful RIVER (p. 107), thirty-five ink drawings, each 27 x 27 inches, unframed, in a continuous wide band which evokes a torrential river. This flow of ink drawings on the wall contrasted with the static monumentality of the two scholars' rocks. The contours the viewer perceives of MOUNTAIN AND RIVER change from far away to close up. Zhang has an affinity with the Chinese saying that "from a distance everything seems static, while up close one perceives movement." Indeed, in MOUNTAIN AND RIVER, from a distance one sees a stable gestalt, the entire gallery installation, while close up one is aware of dynamic configuration of lines and textures and the mobile energy of the forms. The asymmetrical shapes of the rocks, the jagged edges of the larger perforations presents the viewer with changes of perspective, and a beauty from the rocks' internal energy. Zhang's thirty-five works on paper signifying the word "water" in thirty-five different languages give a paradoxical impression both of austerity and sumptuous richness. Areas are activated by swirling calligraphic strokes, in varying shades of white, gray, or black. The artist's virtuosity with ink, which he studied as an art student in Shanghai, recalls the statement of the critic Zhang Yanynam that ink alone can convey all colors: "A good painter is someone who can translate the mind into the fine colors of ink." Zhang insisted on installing the thirty-five drawings without frames, to evoke a continuous river around the gallery, the movement of the drawings in contrast to the stasis of the "mountain" or scholars' rocks.

Why silicone rubber? After Zhang had finished SUMI-INK GARDEN OF RE-CREATION, the artists wrote in his diary:

> I knew I couldn't use materials like wood or plaster. I had seen silicone rubber in high-tech magazines like *Domus* and *Abitare* and found it beautiful. I wanted my next sculptures to be really of this material, a sort of 'postmodern aesthetic shock.'[5]

Zhang does not see art as separate from life, and some works, like FOOTPRINT (1997), reflect the idea that the viewer creates the artwork. FOOTPRINT, of stone, cement, water, sumi-ink, and canvas, had at its center a large cement stone island with concavities of footprints pressed into the cement surface. Water mixed with sumi-ink collects in the footprint concavities. Each visitor is asked to ink their feet and leave their footprints on the canvas floor. Zhang's art reflects his success in finding an artistic vision that contains, reclaims, and fuses Chinese sources into a new identity. What is grandly Chinese is the sumptuous poetry of the space and the way Zhang handles ink.

Zhang's vision of edge and edgelessness extends over into his view of art's relation to life. Fundamental to the artist's mind is the ability to present both cultures without clichés. Considering the formal beauty and cultural relevance of the scholars' rock, it is not surprising that Zhang's recent work re-imagines this enduring archetype of the garden and of Chinese culture.

A signature of his style remains his original and poetic use of displacement, evoking both discordance and harmony. This vision projects into the past and future while celebrating the present. He has that quality T.S. Eliot praised in the artist, "the historic sense, a perception not only of the past but of its presence."

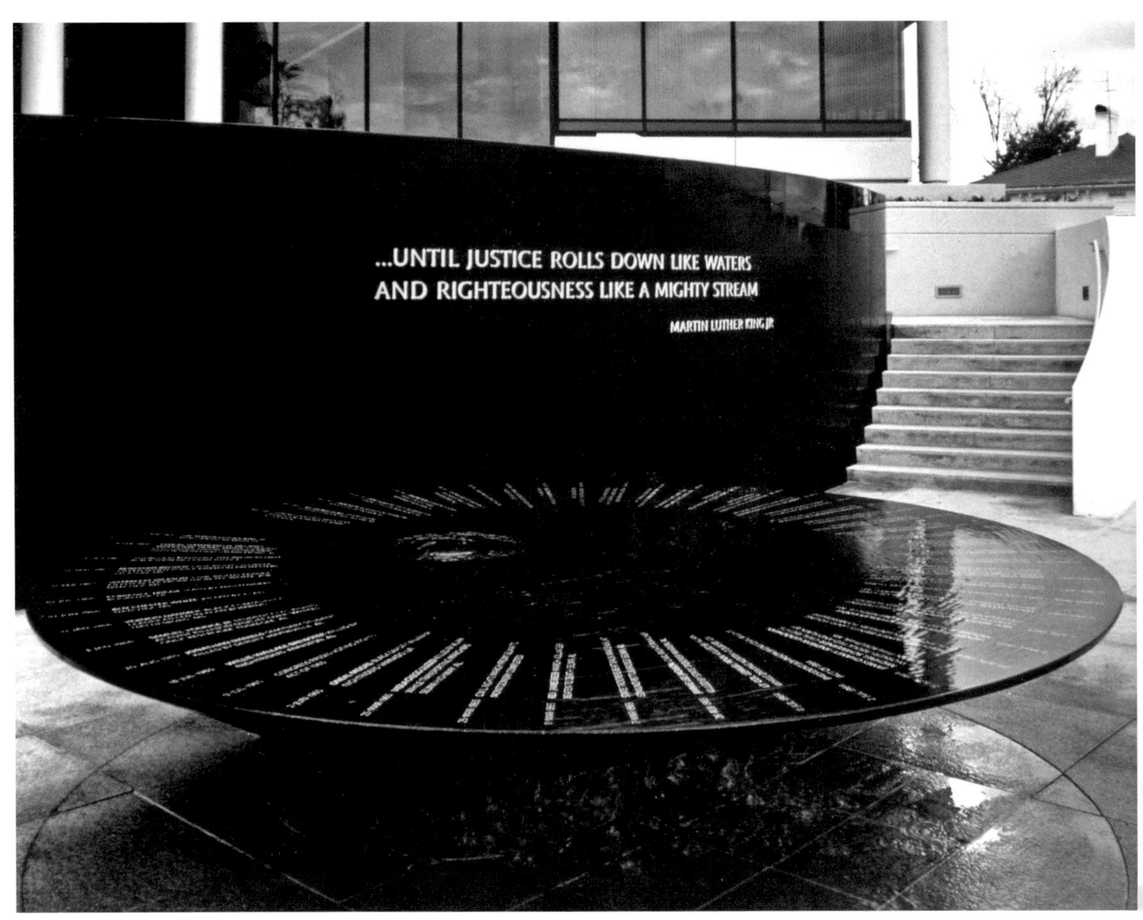


Maya Lin, CIVIL RIGHTS MEMORIAL, 1989

*Chapter XI*

# THE ANTI-CLASSICAL AND THE UNCONTAINED

Classical art and the containing edge are in decline. Sculpture belongs more today to life than to art. Edges that exist, as in Pipilloti Rist, invade space in anarchic ways that challenge the very concept of "edge."

Noguchi's words, voiced in the 1970s, that the electronic age would displace sculpture as man's link to the earth have proven true. Because they seek a dynamic balance between Nature and Art, the contemporary artists I chose for this book perceive our fragmented cosmos yet choose to create sculptural unities. By contrast, most of today's video and installation artists typically choose to create not unity but incoherence, the scattered and the sprawling.

As opposed to a monumental homage to the transient, much of today's art is about a dispersed homage to the non-monumental.

Baudelaire defined beauty as combining the transient and the eternal. It is revealing that the three artists in this book who combine sculpture's permanent and transient values most sharply (stone with water) share an Eastern heritage.

This book has shown the affinity between the life-giving energy of incompleteness, the Zen aesthetic of imperfection, and the mobile, fluctuating contours of contemporary art.

Edges are crucial to the formal aesthetic of art, and the sum of contours creates its unique rhythm. The vitality of rhythm, the artist's orchestration of inner and outer contours defines each artist's style. These artists ask the question: how can a work of art be permanent and also express nature; art, they say, like nature, is incomplete and therein lies its beauty.

Even in the electronic age, edges of art continue to convey art's heightened life, the pulse and energy of beauty. The sculptural edge gives art the dynamism that is inseparable from life.

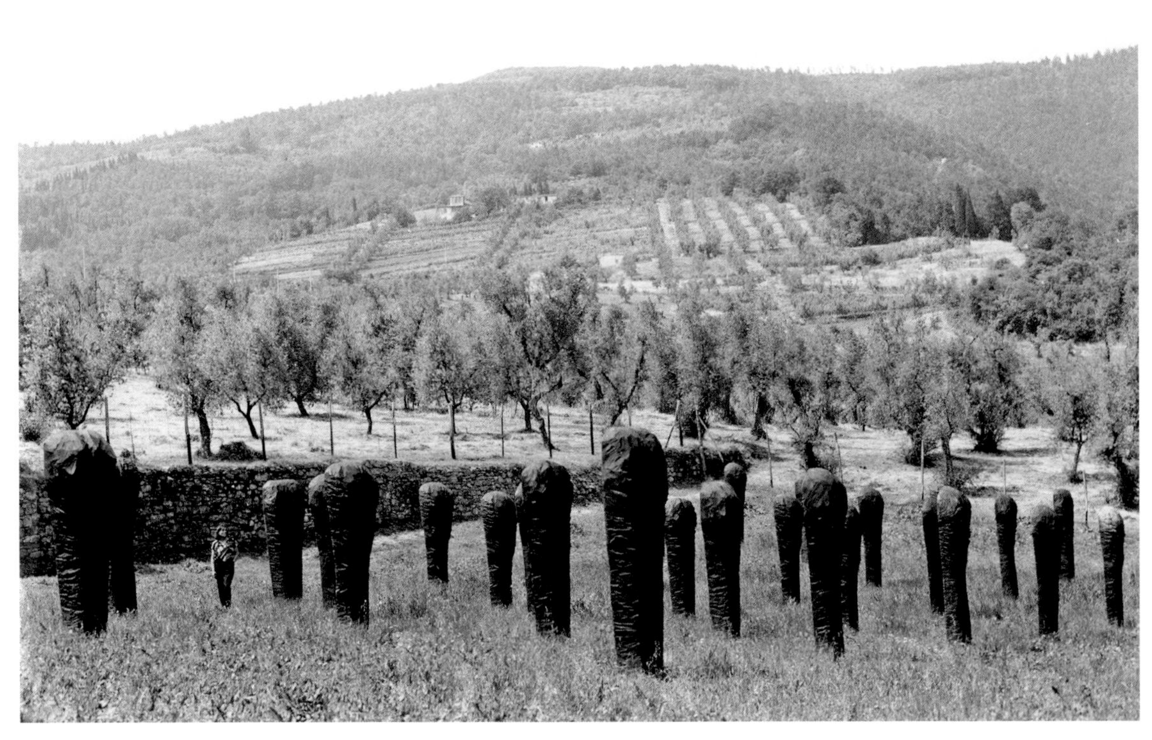

Magdalena Abakanowicz, KATARSIS, 1985

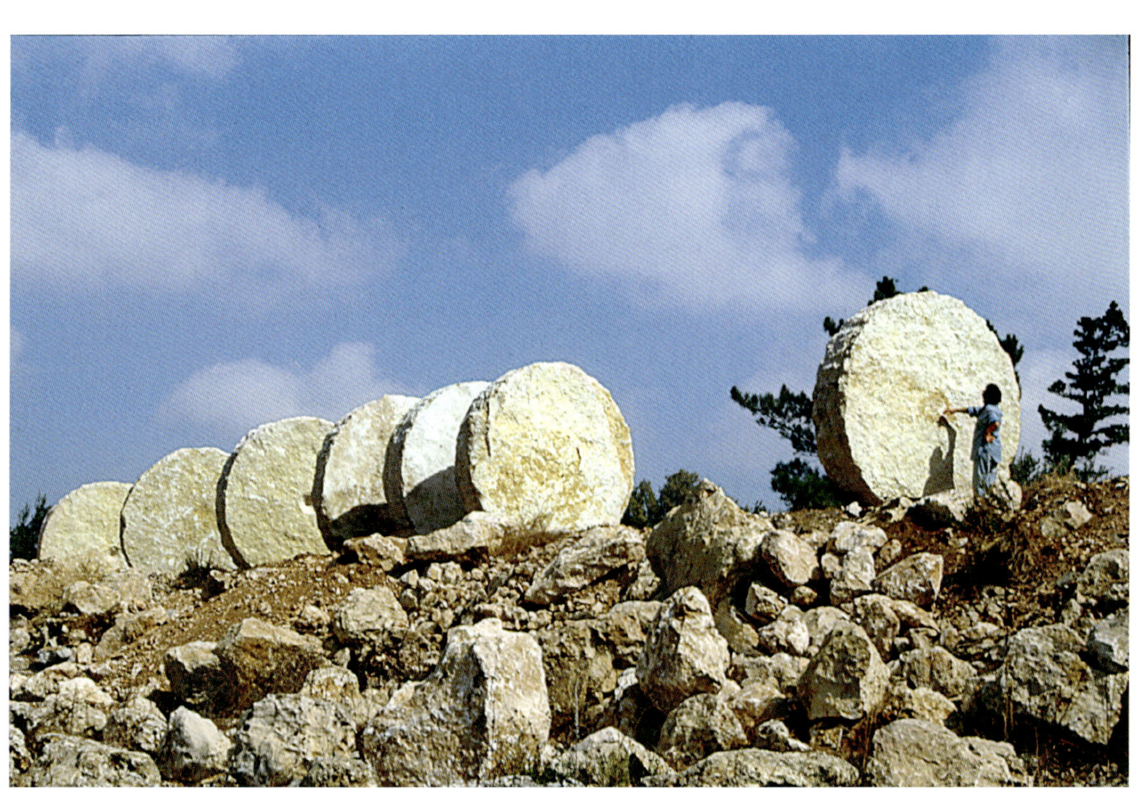

Magdalena Abakanowicz, NEGEV, 1987

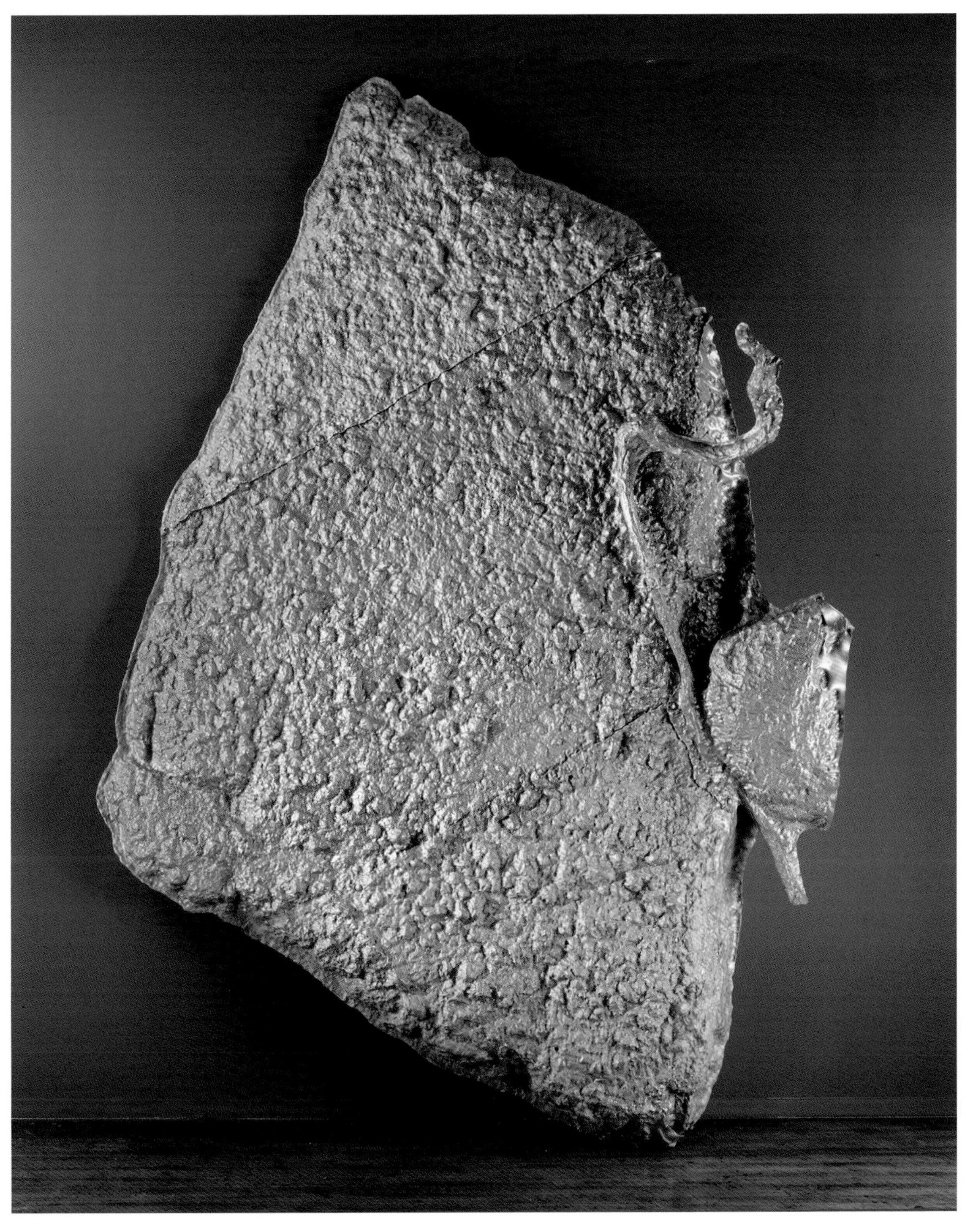

Robert Lobe, VINE, 1999

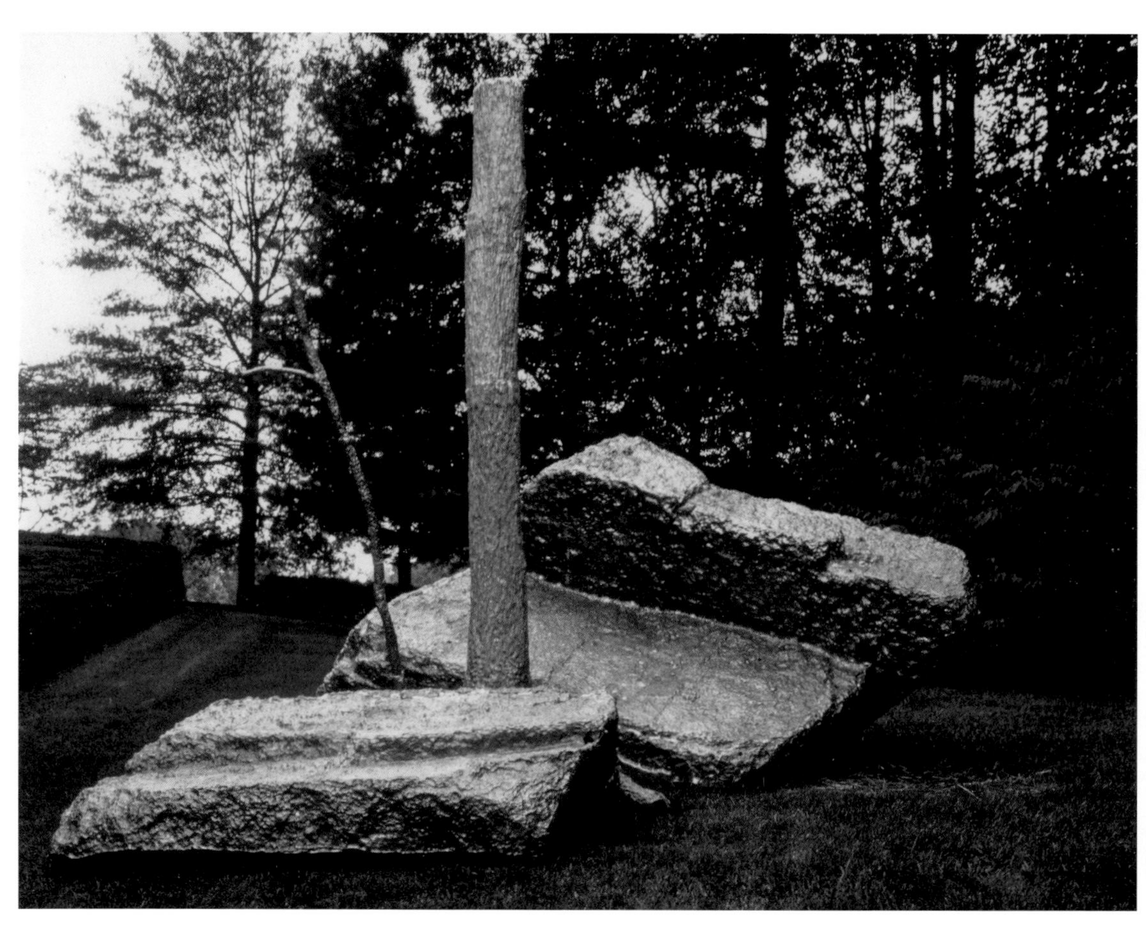

Robert Lobe, HARMONY RIDGE, 1996

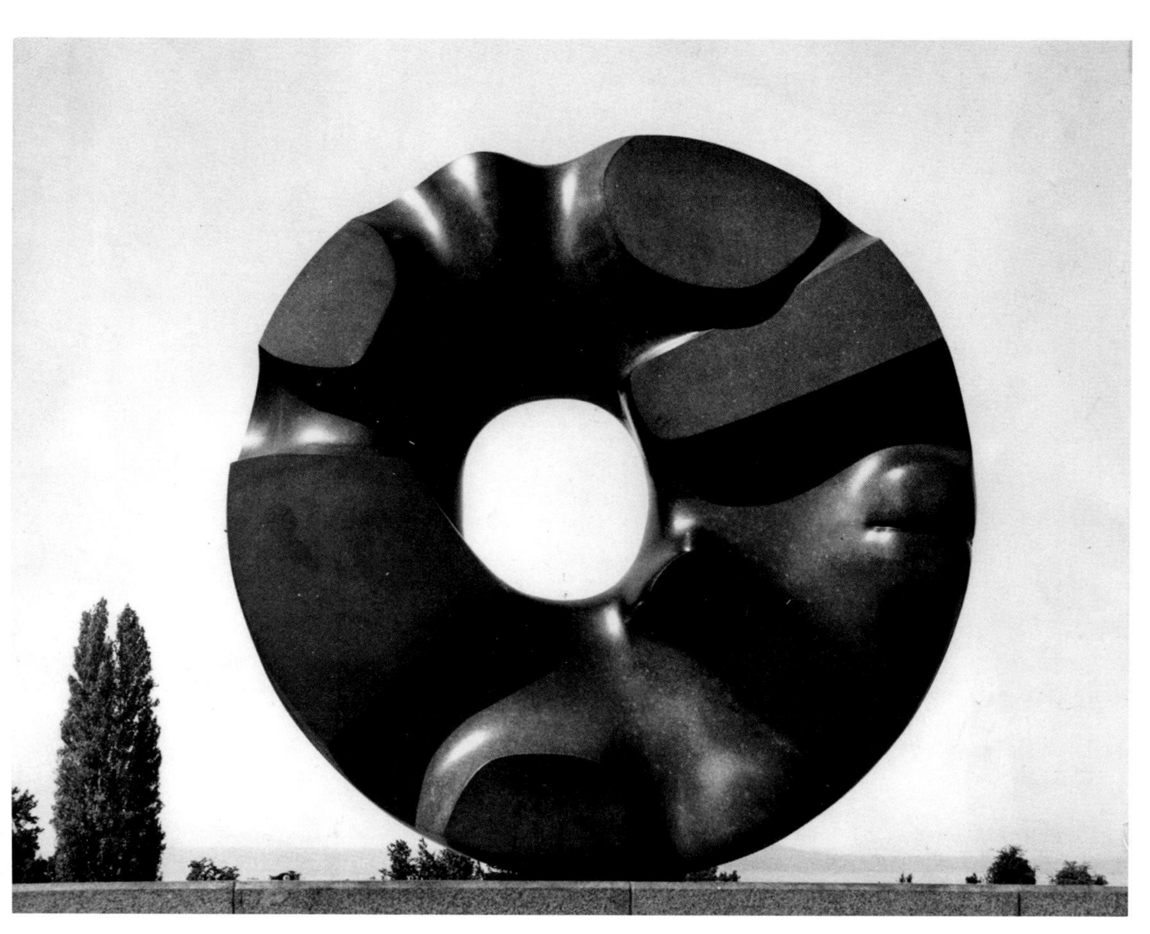

Isamu Noguchi, THE BLACK SUN, 1969

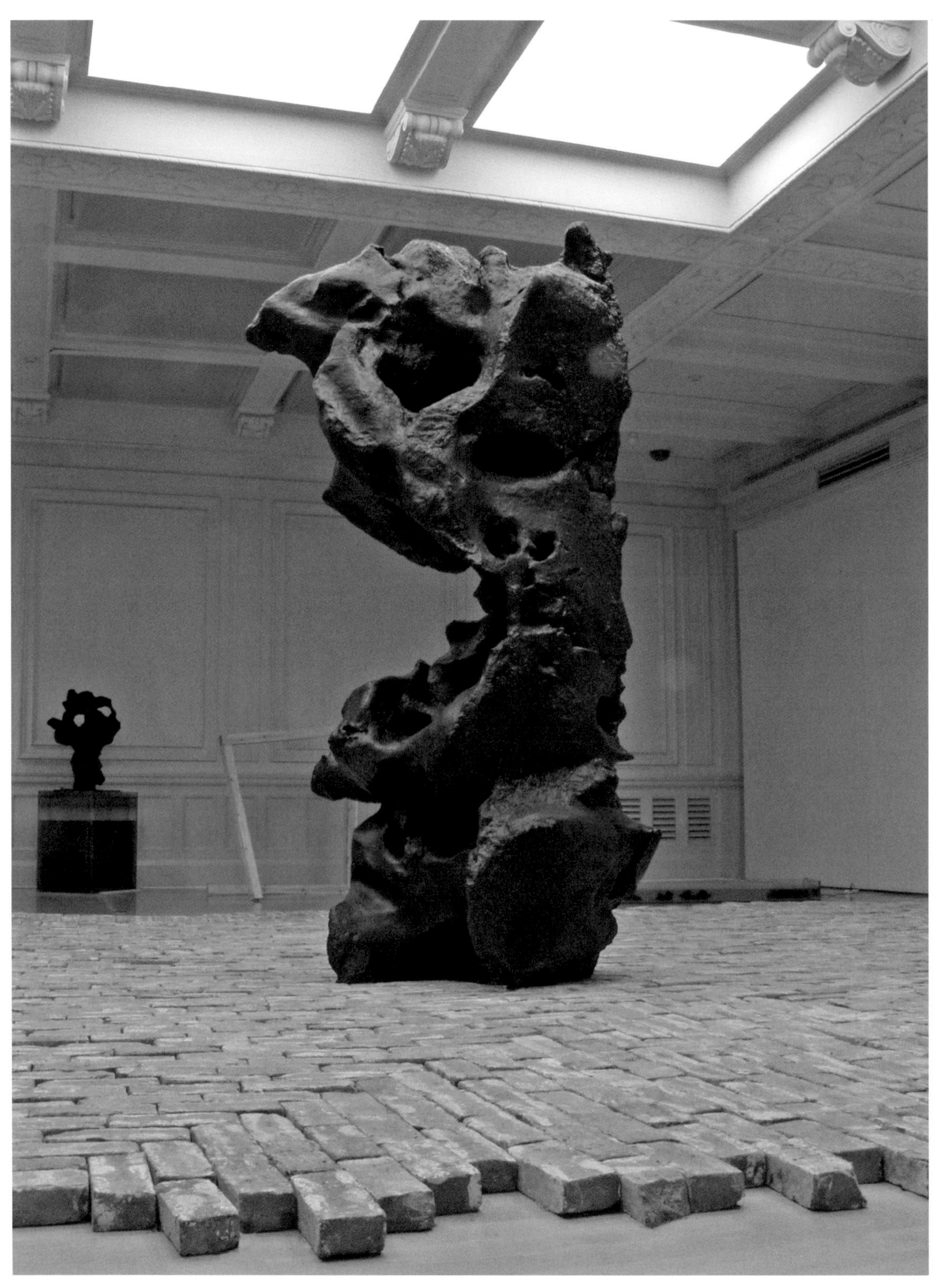

Jian Jun Zhang, SUMI-INK GARDEN OF RE-CREATION, 2002

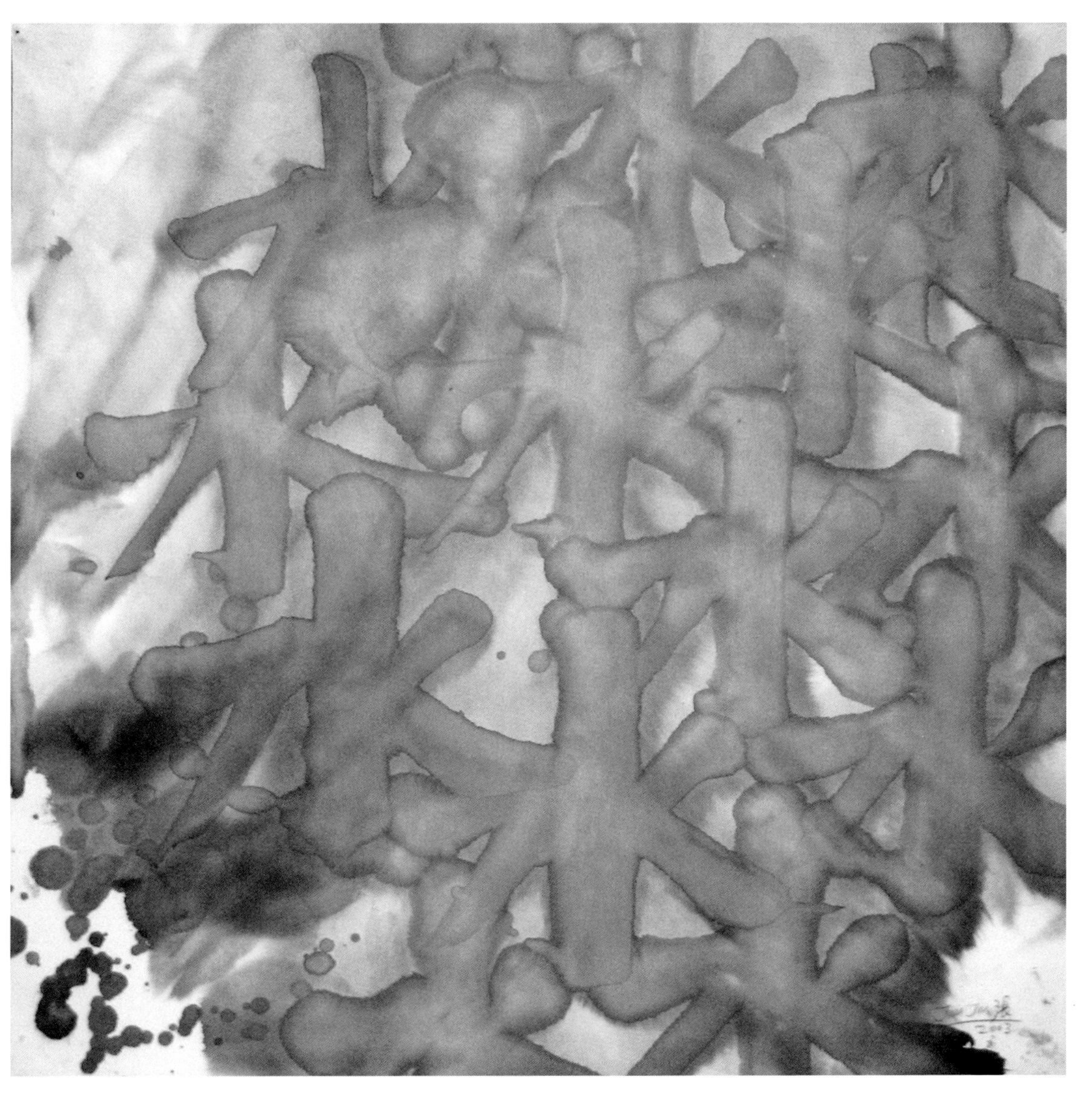

Jian Jun Zhang, RIVER, 2003, detail

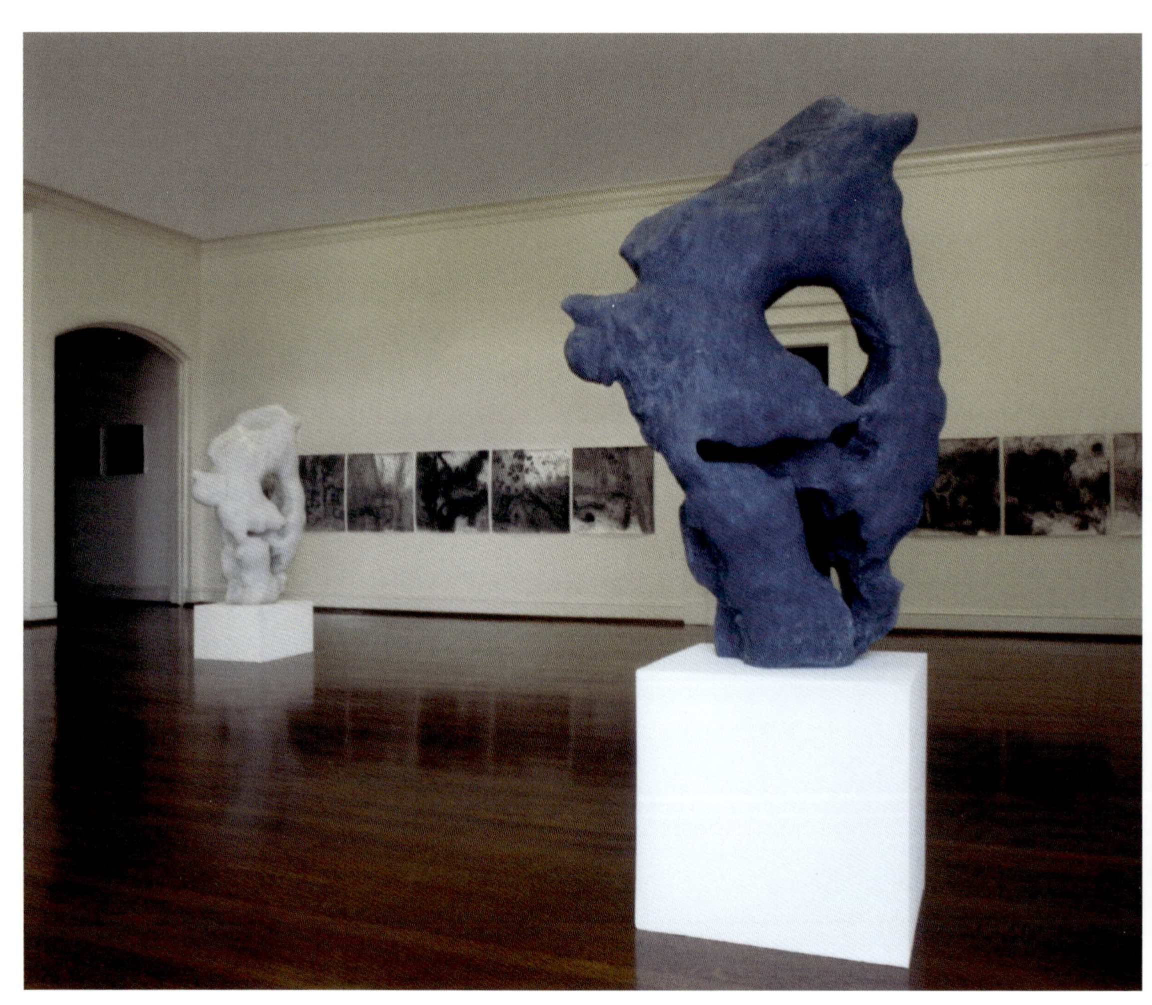

Jian Jun Zhang, MOUNTAIN AND RIVER, 2003

# *Endnotes*

*Chapter I*
EDGE AGAINST SPACE

1. Isamu Noguchi, my interview with the sculptor, February 1980 (see Sheffield, Margaret. "Perfecting the Imperfect: Noguchi's Personal Style," *Artforum*, April 1980, pp. 68–73).
2. For a discussion of asymmetry, irregularity, and imperfection as principles in all the Zen arts, see Hisamatsu, Shinichi. *Zen and the Fine Arts*. Tokyo: Kodansha International, 1971, pp. 29, 83+.
3. Renaissance artists had conceived of a sculpture as being contained spatially by its marble or bronze material. In contrast, a Baroque sculptor like Bernini wanted his work to extend beyond the physical object itself and to dissolve into the surrounding space. In *Apollo and Daphne*, for example, the virtuoso carving of the "edges" of Daphne's fingers creates the illusion that the boundary between the figures and the space around them has been abolished.
4. The issue of the *non-finito*, or "unfinished," in Michelangelo's work has been argued and re-argued continually. One point of view maintains that Michelangelo had intended to finish and polish (at a later date) *St. Matthew* and the *Captives*; this diminishes them as inferior works of art because they were not finished, which at that time meant to polish and smooth with a pumice to eliminate all "uncertain" marks of the chisel.
The opposite point of view, held by scholars John Pope-Hennessy and Charles Avery among others, argues that works by Michelangelo and Donatello were intentionally left unresolved and unfinished and that is precisely the source of their strength and beauty. Pope-Hennessy (in *Italian High Renaissance and Baroque Sculpture*, pp. 13–14) speaks of *St. Matthew*'s new formal rhythms and vastly enhanced tactility and a sense of self-immersion in the sculpture, whereby the statue was no longer something external to himself but a projection of his total personality. Charles Avery (in *Donatello*, p. 107) argues that Donatello's reliefs of St. Lawrence look as if they were left rough and unfinished "deliberately, as a means of expression."
To me, the unresolved quality of *St. Matthew* or the *Captives* reflects the dark poetry of Michelangelo's passionate mind. After all, Michelangelo famously had described the process of carving marble as the freeing of the figure from its block by removing excess stone. What better visual metaphor for captivity than a sculpture still "imprisoned" in its stone block? In the late *Pietà* figures or *St. Matthew*, "roughness" is part of the subject matter, whether it means intense suffering or spiritual struggle.
Meyer Schapiro, in his essay "On Perfection, Coherence and the Unity of Form and Content" (1966) insists that "certain kinds of incompleteness and irresolution can be precisely the elements that impart to sculpture that life-enhancing energy."
For Maya Lin, Giuseppe Penone, and Jian Jun Zhang, the idea of the incomplete is an important aspect both of the content and of the style of each artist. The empty spaces in Penone's wire-mesh cages in *Respirare Ombra* (2003) are continually completing themselves or are in a stage of becoming. Likewise in Zhang's *Sumi-Ink Garden of Re-creation* (2002) part of the work included cast "stones" made of ink and resin that were gradually eroded by water.
This concept of the "incomplete" is central to this book, with different contexts and nuances of meaning, in the work not only of Michelangelo, where it is often called the *non-finito*, but also in the work of Noguchi (the imperfect and the deliberately unfinished as being closer to the truth of nature, the incomplete or rough edge as reaching beyond the apparent boundary into the infinite), Maya Lin, Penone, Jian Jun Zhang, and, in the present, artists like Pipillotti Rist.
5. "I first look at the front, the back, and the two profiles. Then I do the intermediates, which means three-quarter profiles. And then I do it again, producing profiles that are tighter and tighter, cleaning them up, as the human body has an infinite number of profiles. I do as many as I

can, and need to." Auguste Rodin, in an interview with Henri Dujardin-Beaumetz, translated by Albert Elsen, in *Auguste Rodin: Readings on his Life and Work*. Englewood Cliffs, NJ: Prentice Hall, 1965, p. 139.
6. Schapiro, Meyer. "On Perfection, Coherence and the Unity of Form and Content," *Op.cit.*, p. 47.
7. Noguchi saw water as a physical and symbolic material in his sculpture. Like the water basins and fountains in Japanese gardens, water instills a meditative and eternal mood. Even in a work in an urban setting such as the Chase Manhattan Bank Plaza, Noguchi noted with pleasure that, as he had planned, the Chase garden "floods in the summer with water cascading over its rim." In *Water Stone* (1987), the water reaches the surface of the basalt due to it flowing up into the basin and then over the rim, affirming once again water's transience and mobility versus the permanence of stone.
8. Webster's Third New International Dictionary. This meaning of edge is precisely what is meant by the Japanese word *hashi*. "*Ma* divides the world. Originally the word *hashi* referred not only to a bridge, but also to an edge, chopsticks, steps. The word *hashi* did not mean a specific thing, but implied the bridging of '*ma*.'" (In Isozaki, Arata. *MA – Space-Time in Japan*. New York: Cooper-Hewitt, 1978.)
9. Golding, John. "Under Cézanne's Spell," *The New York Review of Books*, January 11, 1996.
10. Hughes, Robert. *Nothing If Not Critical*. New York: Penguin Books, 1987, p. 185.
11. Herder, Johann Gottfried. *Sculpture*. Chicago: The University of Chicago Press, 2002, p. 33.
12. Elsen, *Op. cit.*, p. 83: "To obtain light, Rodin emphasized the role of holes and edges in his work. To look for form in nature and bring out grace, vigor, amorous charm, or the untamed fire, by taking form amplifying it, exaggerating the holes and lumps so as to give them more light." On the *Burghers of Calais*: "Within an area confirmed by a few inches of the sculpture, each fingertip will encounter surface inflections of a different character: feeling one's own arm, one gets the impression that the surfaces conceived by Rodin are more richly complex. Only when one inserts the hand into the furrowed backs or deep socketed eyes of the sculpture can the mind be convinced of what the eye has seen."
13. Perl, Jed. *Eyewitness: Reports from an Art World in Crisis*. New York: Basic Books, 2000, p. 318. Perl's description of the viewer's perception of Chardin's *The Brioche* speaks of the multiplying complexity of Chardin's compositional structure, "a dream of unity that we glimpse through an atmosphere saturated by particularities." These words precisely apply to the function of the varied edges within a work of sculpture.
14. Isozaki, see note 8.
15. Quoted in Spurling, Hilary. *The Unknown Matisse – A Life of Henry Matisse. The Early Years, 1869–1908*. New York: Alfred A. Knopf, 1998, p. 313.
16. See note 4.
17. Author interview with Magdalena Abakanowicz, February 2002.

### *Chapter II*
### THE BAROQUE: GIANLORENZO BERNINI

1. Simon Schama in *Landscape and Memory*. New York: Alfred A. Knopf, 1995, p. 292.
2. Ibid., p. 292: "In other words, Bernini took comedy seriously, even in the dramatic pieces he wrote for the theater of the Palazzo Barberini, which combined light, music, and startling effects in a conscious effort to negate the boundary between audience and performance."
In one play, *The Flooding of the Tiber*, he went so far as to have water gush from the back of the stage towards the front rows, only to be diverted at the last moment by a canal, hidden from the public sight line.
3. Chantelou, Paul Freart de. *Diary of the Cavaliere Bernini's Visit to France*, edited and introduced by Anthony Blunt. Princeton: Princeton University Press, 1985.

4. Avery, Charles. *Bernini: Genius of the Baroque.* Boston: Bullfinch Press, 1997, p. 262; Baldinucci, Filippo. *The Life of Bernini.* Translated by Catherine and Robert Enggass. University Park, PA: Pennsylvania State University Press, 1966.
5. Wolfflin, Heinrich. *Renaissance and Baroque.* Ithaca, NY: Cornell University Press, 1991, pp. 62–70. Wolfflin notes of the oval in Baroque art: "The circle is for instance an absolutely static and unchangeable form, but the oval is restless and always seems on the point of change . . . the Baroque had achieved its purpose by means of the irregular and apparently incomplete, the unsettled and impermanent form . . ."

*Chapter III*
TRANSITIONAL GIANT:
AUGUSTE RODIN

1. "To look for form in Nature and bring out grace, vigor , amorous charm, or the untamed fire by taking form, amplifying it, exaggerating the holes and bumps so as to give them more light. after which I search for a synthesis of the whole." In Goldwater, Robert. *What is Modern Sculpture?* New York: Museum of Modern Art, 1965, p. 34.
2. Lampert, Catherine. *Rodin: Sculpture & Drawings.* London: Arts Council of Great Britain, 1986, p. 28.
3. Quoted in Ibid., p. 31.
4. Elsen, *Op. cit.*, pp. 165–166.
5. Ibid., p. 172.
6. Henry Moore, from "Henry Moore Parle de Rodin," *L'OEIL*, November 1967, p. 63.
7. Lampert, Catherine. *Rodin: Sculpture & Drawings, Op. cit.*, p. 166.
8. Ibid., p. 170.

*Chapter IV*
FUTURISM:
UMBERTO BOCCIONI

1. Umberto Boccioni, "Technical Manifesto of Futurist Sculpture, 1912," Herschel B. Chipp, *Theories of Modern Art.* Chicago: University of Chicago Press, 1968, p. 298 (fifth printing). Originally published on April 11, 1912. This translation was made from the volume of collected manifestoes, *I Manifesti del Futurismo,* edited by Marinetti, and is from *Futurism* by Joshua C. Taylor, The Museum of Modern Art, New York, 1961, and reprinted with its permission. The above translation is by Richard Chase. Boccioni published the manifesto and the preface to the catalogue of his sculpture exhibition in Paris (Galerie La Boetie, June 20 – July 16, 1913), in his *Pittura scultura futurista.* Milan: Poesia, 1914, pp. 391–411, 413–421.
2. Umberto Boccioni in Herschel B. Chipp, *Theories of Modern Art, Op. cit.*, p. 298. "Technical Manifesto of Futurist Sculpture, 1912," translation by Richard Chase.
3. F. T. Marinetti, "Technical Manifesto, 11 April, 1911," ibid., p. 289.
4. Paul Klee, "Creative Credo, 1920," ibid., p. 182. Originally published in *Schopferische Konfession,* ed. Kasimir Edschmid (Berlin: Erich Reisee, 1920) (Tribune der Kunst und Zeit, No. 13). This English translation by Norbert Guterman from the *Inward Vision: Watercolors, Drawings, and Writings by Paul Klee.* New York: Abrams, 1959, pp. 5–10.

*Chapter V*
ISAMU NOGUCHI

1. Altshuler, Bruce. *Noguchi.* New York: Abbeville Press, 1994, p. 31: "Continuous aesthetic judgments affect even the control of our emotions, bringing order out of chaos, a myth out of the world, a sense of belonging out of our loneliness."
2. Ibid., p. 58: "In the circular water garden at Chase Manhattan Bank Plaza in New York, the seven elements were 'fished' from the Uji River near Kyoto, river stones of fantastic shape . . . I can see that looking down into the garden with its water flowing will be like looking into a

turbulent seascape from which immobile rocks take off for outer space."
3. Author's interview with Noguchi, February 1980.
4. Ibid.
5. Arata Izozaki, *Ma: Space Time in Japan*. New York: Cooper-Hewitt, 1978.

### *Chapter VI*
### MAGDALENA ABAKANOWICZ

1. Interview with the artist, October 2003.
2. Magdalena Abakanowicz, statement of 1978, reprinted in Magdalena Abakanowicz, exhibition catalogue (Chicago, Museum of Contemporary Art in Association with Abbeyville Publishers, 1982), p. 94. The artist speaks of the delicate edges of fibers which she sees as the basic element in the organic world of our planet.
3. Abakanowicz's statement in Acceptance Speech for Lifetime Achievement Award from the International Sculpture Center, Washington, D.C., 2005. "What is sculpture? With impressive continuity it testifies to man's evolving sense of reality, and fulfills the necessity to express what cannot be verbalized. Banished from paradise, man found himself confronted by the space of the world. It was a territory unknown and inconceivable, as inconceivable as are overabundance and emptiness. He tried to reach unknown powers, raising stones, building areas of special meaning. Sculpture became the language beyond words. Today we are confronted with the inconceivable world we ourselves created. Its reality is reflected in art."
4. Barbara Rose, *Magdalena Abakanowicz*. New York: Harry N. Abrams, 1994, p. 72.
5. Ibid., p. 100.
6. Ibid., p. 105.
7. Ibid., p. 105.
8. Interview with the artist, also quoted in Hunter Drohojowska, "Magical Mystery Tours," *Art News*, 54, September 1985, p. 112.

### *Chapter VII*
### MAYA LIN: THE EDGE AS POETIC IDEA

1. Maya Lin, *Boundaries*. New York: Simon and Schuster, 2000. Chapter on *Vietnam Veterans Memorial*.
2. Ibid., chapter of *Boundaries* on *Vietnam Veterans Memorial*.
3. Ibid., chapter of *Boundaries* on the artist's childhood and biography.
4. Ibid., chapter of *Boundaries* on *Vietnam Veterans Memorial*.
5. Holland Cotter, "Once Inspired by the War, now Inspired by the Land," *The New York Times*, May 8, 2009.
6. Press release from STORM KING WAVEFIELD, words of the artist, March 2009, p. 1.
7. Maya Lin, *Boundaries, Op.cit.*, Chapter on *Civil Rights Memorial*.

NB: There are no pages numbers in *Boundaries*, only chapter headings.

### *Chapter VIII*
### ROBERT LOBE: THE BAROQUE ABSTRACT

1. Interview with the artist, 2003.
2. Ibid.
3. Ibid.
4. Michael Brenson, "The Landscape Maintains Its Hold on American Artists," *The New York Times*, March 8, 1986. Brenson noted the "danger and distance" with which Americans viewed nature.
5. Lobe has pointed out an affinity in the destructiveness of his work and his use of industrial materials to the art of John Chamberlain.

## *Chapter IX*
## GIUSEPPE PENONE: THE BREATH, THE TOUCH, THE TREE

1.Catherine de Zegher, curator and editor, *Giuseppe Penone: The Imprint of Drawing.* New York: The Drawing Center, 2004. Essays by Catherine de Zegher, Briony Fer, Michael Newman, Kathryn Tuma, Giuseppe Penone. "If the Duchampian anti-retinal project had sought to defy sculpture, Penone's tactile diagrams vastly expand the idea of sculpture to chart even the slightest sensory experience, as if it were an intricate 'map of the pressure points' between skin and surface," p. 94.

NB: All other quotes in this chapter are taken from the above-mentioned text.

## *Chapter X*
## JIAN JUN ZHANG

1. Conference, moderated by Xian Min Zhang, at the China Institute, New York, May 14, 2009, for artists born in China who are now living and working both in China and in New York.
2. Chapter on Jian Jun Zhang by Margaret Sheffield for book entitled *Art Projects International: Ten Years.* New York: Art Projects International, 2003, pp. 70-83.
3. Interview with the artist, October 2008.
4. Conversation with the artist, March 19, 2009.
5. Interview with the artist, March 19, 2009.

## *List of Works*

Isamu Noguchi, LANDSCAPE SCULPTURE, late 1960s
black granite, diameter approx. 40"
© Isamu Noguchi Foundation
© Artist Rights Society (ARS), New York
p. 23

KRITIOS BOY from the Acropolis, ca. 490–480 BCE
marble, height 46"
Acropolis Museum, Athens, Greece
© Nimatallah/Art Resource
p. 25

Aristide Maillol, THE MEDITERRANEAN, 1902–1905 (cast 1951–1953)
bronze, 41" x 45" x 29 3/4" including base
The Museum of Modern Art, New York
© Artist Rights Society (ARS), New York
© The Museum of Modern Art/ Licensed by SCALA/ Art Resource, New York
p. 27

Gianlorenzo Bernini, APOLLO AND DAPHNE, detail, 1622–1625
marble, height 95 3/4"
Galleria Borghese, Rome, Italy
© Alinari/Art Resource, New York
p. 28

Auguste Rodin, MIGNON, 1867–1868 (cast 1925)
bronze, 15 1/2" x 12" x 19 1/2"
Rodin Museum, Philadelphia
© The Philadelphia Museum of Art/Art Resource, New York
p. 29

Michelangelo Buonarroti, ST. MATTHEW, ca. 1506
marble, height 106 3/4"
Accademia, Florence, Italy
© Alinari/Art Resource, New York
p. 30

Michelangelo Buonarroti, CAPTIVE, 1519
marble, 92 1/2"
Accademia, Florence, Italy
© Alinari/Art Resource, New York
p. 31

Michelangelo Buonarotti, RONDANINI PIETÀ, 1564
marble, height 76 3/4"
Castello Sforzesco, Milan
© Alinari/Art Resource, New York
p. 33

Gianlorenzo Bernini, APOLLO AND DAPHNE (detail of Daphne's hair)
© Alinari/Art Resource, New York
p. 34

Auguste Rodin, L'HOMME QUI MARCHE, 1877–1878 (cast 1917)
bronze, height 33 1/4"
Musee Rodin, Paris
© Vanni/Art Resource, NY
p. 40

Benvenuto Cellini, PERSEUS, 1545–1553
bronze, height 124"
Loggia dei Lanzi, Florence
© Archive Timothy McCarthy/Art Resource, New York
p. 57

Phidias, RIACE WARRIOR (A), ca. 460 BCE
bronze, height 78 3/4"
Museo Archeologico Nazionale, Reggio Calabria
© Erich Lessing/Art Resource, New York
p. 59

Giuseppe Penone, SCRIGNO, 2007
leather, 20' x 9'
Photo: Francesca Mannoni
© Artist Rights Society (ARS), New York
p. 61

Magdalena Abakanowicz, SPACE OF STONE, 2002
Barre grey granite and black Pennsylvania granite
22 elements, 152" x 2172" x 828"
Grounds for Sculpture, Hamilton, New Jersey
© Magdalena Abakanowicz,
courtesy Marlborough Gallery, New York
p. 62

Maya Lin, WAVEFIELD, 1995
earth and grass, approx. 10,000' sq.
FXB Aerospace Building, University of Michigan, Ann Arbor, Michigan
© Kevin Fitzsimmons
© University of Michigan Photo Services
© Maya Lin Studio, Inc.,
courtesy PaceWildenstein, New York
p. 68

Robert Lobe, PAGE I, VOL. 11, 1999
anodized hammered aluminum, 60" x 39" x 10"
© the artist
p. 79

Gianlorenzo Bernini, DAVID, 1623–1624
marble, 67"
Galleria Borghese, Rome
© Alinari/Art Resource, New York
p. 80

Gianlorenzo Bernini, FOUNTAIN OF THE FOUR RIVERS, detail, 1651
marble, over life-sized
Piazza Navona, Rome
© Alinari/Art Resource, New York
p. 81

Gianlorenzo Bernini, LOUIS XIV, 1665
marble, height 31 1/2"
Musée National de Versailles, Versailles
© Alinari/Art Resource, New York
p. 83

Umberto Boccioni, UNIQUE FORMS OF CONTINUITY IN SPACE, 1913
bronze, 48" x 15 1/2" x 36"
Metropolitan Museum of Art, New York
© Art Resource, New York
p. 84

Isamu Noguchi, VERTICAL VIEW, late 1960s
granite and mihara, 41 1/4" x 41 1/4" x 30 1/8"
Noguchi Museum, Long Island City, New York
© Isamu Noguchi Foundation
© Artist Rights Society (ARS), New York
p. 85

Giuseppe Penone, RESPIRARE OMBRA, 2003
488 wire-mesh boxes filled with laurel, 52' long
© Marian Goodman Gallery, New York
© Artist Rights Society (ARS), New York
p. 86

Maya Lin, CIVIL RIGHTS MEMORIAL, 1989
black granite
The Southern Poverty Law Center, Montgomery, Alabama
© Norman McGrath
© Southern Poverty Law Center
© Maya Lin Studio, Inc.,
courtesy PaceWildenstein, New York
p. 98

Magdalena Abakanowicz, KATARSIS, 1985
22 bronze figures
Villa Celle Sculpture Park, Pistoia, Italy
© Magdalena Abakanowicz,
courtesy Marlborough Gallery, New York
p. 100

Magdalena Abakanowicz, NEGEV, 1987
7 limestone disks, 120" in diameter x 30" in depth, each weighing 12 tons
Limestone from the Negev Desert, Israel
Billy Rose Sculpture Garden, Jerusalem
© Magdalena Abakanowicz,
courtesy Marlborough Gallery, New York
p. 101

Robert Lobe, VINE, 1999
Anodized hammered aluminum, 123 1/2 x 82 1/2 x 31"
Photo: the artist
p. 103

Robert Lobe, HARMONY RIDGE, 1996
anodized hammered aluminum,
approx. 12' x 14' x 17'
US Geological Survey Reston Virginia
p. 104

Isamu Noguchi, THE BLACK SUN, 1969
Brazilian granite, height 96"
Seattle Art Museum, Seattle, Washington
© Isamu Noguchi Foundation
© Artist Rights Society (ARS), New York
p. 105

Jian Jun Zhang, SUMI-INK GARDEN OF RE-CREATION, 2002
sumi-ink, bricks, water, fish, height 9'
© the artist
p. 106

Jian Jun Zhang, RIVER, 2003, detail
35 panels of sumi-ink on rice paper, each panel 27" x 27"
© the artist
p. 107

Jian Jun Zhang, MOUNTAIN AND RIVER, 2003, installation view
MOUNTAIN: silicon rubber, height 48"
RIVER: 35 Panels of sumi-ink on rice paper, each 27" x 27"
© the artist
p. 108

## *Bibliography*

Als, Hilton (foreword). *Drawing Us In: How We Experience Visual Art*. Deborah Chasman and Edna Chiang (eds.). Boston: Beacon Press, 2000.

Altshuler, Bruce. *Noguchi*. New York: Abbeville Press, 1994.

Altshuler, Bruce and Diane Apostolos-Cappadona (eds.). *Isamu Noguchi: Essays and Conversations*. New York: Harry N. Abrams in conjunction with The Isamu Noguchi Foundation, 1994.

Ashton, Dore. *Noguchi: East and West*. New York: Alfred A. Knopf, 1992.

Ashton, Dore and Carmen Gimenez. *Picasso and the Age of Iron*. New York: Solomon R. Guggenheim Foundation, 1993.

Avery, Charles. *Bernini: Genius of the Baroque*. Boston: Bullfinch Press, 1997.

Avery, Charles. *Donatello: An Introduction*. New York: Icon Editions, 1994.

Awakawa, Yasuichi. *Zen Painting*. Tokyo: Kondansha International, 1970.

Baldinucci, Filippo. *The Life of Bernini*. Translated by Catherine and Robert Enggass. University Park, PA: Pennsylvania State University Press, 1966.

Chantelou, Paul Freart de. *Diary of the Cavaliere Bernini's Visit to France*, edited and introduced by Anthony Blunt. Princeton: Princeton University Press, 1985.

Clark, Kenneth. *The Nude*. London: Penguin Books, 1956.

Cotter, Holland. "Where the Ocean Meets the Catskills," *The New York Times*, May 8, 2009.

Drexler, Arthur. *The Architecture of Japan*. New York: The Museum of Modern Art, 1955.

Elsen, Albert. *Auguste Rodin: Readings on His Life and Work*. Englewood Cliffs, NJ: Prentice Hall, 1965.

Fry, Roger. *Vision and Design*. New York: Brentano Publishers, 1925.

Golding, John. "Under Cézanne's Spell," *The New York Review of Books*, January 11, 1996.

Goldwater, Robert. *What Is Modern Sculpture?* New York: Museum of Modern Art, 1965.

Hayashiya, T. *Japanese Arts and the Tea Ceremony*. New York: John Weatherhill, 1994.

Herder, Johann Gottfried. *Sculpture*. Chicago: The University of Chicago Press, 2002.
Herrmann-Fiore, Kristina. *Apollo e Dafne del Bernini nella Galleria Borghese*. Milan: Silvana Editoriale, 1997.
Hest, Barbara. *Lucio Fontana*. Cologne: Taschen, 2006.
Hisamatsu, Shinichi. *Zen and the Fine Arts*. Tokyo: Kodansha International, 1971.
Hughes, Robert. *Nothing If Not Critical*. New York: Penguin Books, 1987.
Hunter, Sam. *Isamu Noguchi*. New York: Abbeville Press, 1978.
Isozaki, Arata. *MA – Space-Time in Japan*. New York: Cooper-Hewitt, 1978.
Itoh, Teiji. *Japanese Garden: An Approach to Nature*. New Haven: Yale University Press, 1972.
Kim, Sheila. "Maya Lin Unveils Her Environmentally Sensitive 'Storm King Wavefield,'" *Interior Design*, March 25, 2009.
Krauss, Rosalind. *Passages in Modern Sculpture*. New York: Viking Press, 1977.
Kuck, Loraine. *The World of the Japanese Garden*. Tokyo: John Weatherhill, 1968.
Lampert, Catherine. *Rodin: Sculpture & Drawings*. London: Arts Council of Great Britain, 1986.
Lin, Maya. *Boundaries*. New York: Simon and Schuster, 2000.
Mori, Osamu. *Typical Japanese Gardens*. Tokyo: Japan Publications Co., 1962.
Mori, Osamu and Irmtraus Schaaschmidt-Richter. *Japanese Gardens*. New York: William Morrow, 1979.
Noguchi, Isamu. *The Isamu Noguchi Museum*. New York: Harry N. Abrams, 1987.
Noguchi, Isamu. *A Sculptor's World*. New York: Harper & Row, 1968.
Perl, Jed. *Eyewitness: Reports from an Art World in Crisis*. New York: Basic Books, 2000.
Phelan, Peggy et al. *Pipilotti Rist*. New York: Phaidon, 2001.
Pope-Hennessy, John. *Italian High Renaissance and Baroque Sculpture*. New York: Vintage Books, 1985.
Rose, Barbara. *Magdalena Abakanowicz*. New York: Harry N. Abrams, 1994.
Rossi, Laura Mattioli. *Boccioni's Materia: A Futurist Masterpiece and the Avant-Garde in Milan and Paris*. New York: Solomon R. Guggenheim Foundation, 2004.
Schama, Simon. *Landscape and Memory*. New York: Alfred A. Knopf, 1995.
Schapiro, Meyer. *Modern Art: 19th and 20th Centuries*. New York: George Braziller, 1979.
Schapiro, Meyer. "On Perfection, Coherence, and Unity of Form and Content," in Meyer Schapiro, *Theory and Philosophy of Art: Style, Artist, and Society*. New York: George Braziller, 1994.
Scigliano, Eric. *Michelangelo's Mountain*. New York: Free Press, 2005.
Spurling, Hilary. *The Unknown Matisse – A Life of Henry Matisse. The Early Years, 1869–1908*. New York: Alfred A. Knopf, 1998.
Tisdall, Caroline and Angelo Bozzolla. *Futurism*. New York: Thames and Hudson, 1997.
Tucker, William. *The Language of Sculpture*. New York: Thames and Hudson, 1974.
Wittkover, Rudolf. *Bernini*. London: The Phaidon Press, 1966.
Wolfflin, Heinrich. *Renaissance and Baroque*. Ithaca, NY: Cornell University Press, 1991.
Zegher, Catherine de. *Giuseppe Penone: The Imprint of Drawing*. New York: The Drawing Center, 2004.

## *Author's Biographical Note*

Margaret Sheffield is an art critic, curator, and scholar. As a Professor of English Literature she has taught literature and writing at New York University, the New School, and Bard College. She has published articles on art for *The New York Times*, *Artforum*, *Art in America*, *Connoisseur*, and *Sculpture Magazine*. She lived in Rome and Florence for five years. She learned about the aesthetic of transience from Isamu Noguchi and the aesthetic of permanence from the sculpture of Italy.

To find out more about Charta,
and to learn about our most recent publications,
visit

www.chartaartbooks.it

Printed in October 2009
by Tipografia Rumor, Vicenza
for Edizioni Charta